FOCU$ ON
FINANCIAL
MANAGEMENT

FOCU$ ON
FINANCIAL
MANAGEMENT

Ivan K. Cohen

Richmond, the American International
University in London

ICP

Imperial College Press

Published by

Imperial College Press
57 Shelton Street
Covent Garden
London WC2H 9HE

Distributed by

World Scientific Publishing Co. Pte. Ltd.
5 Toh Tuck Link, Singapore 596224
USA office: 27 Warren Street, Suite 401-402, Hackensack, NJ 07601
UK office: 57 Shelton Street, Covent Garden, London WC2H 9HE

British Library Cataloguing-in-Publication Data
A catalogue record for this book is available from the British Library.

FOCUS ON FINANCIAL MANAGEMENT

ISBN   1-86094-479-5

Printed in Singapore.

This book is dedicated to those who came before, and to those who follow on.

Firstly, this book is dedicated to the memory of my late father, Issy (Israel) Cohen *z"l*, and my beloved mother, Irene Cohen. Together they brought me up to be a *mensch*, and their love and support has enabled me to live a fulfilling life without giving up on fun.

Secondly, this book is dedicated to my two children, David Jonathan (Yoni) and Maya Isabella, whose energy and vitality keep me going even as they run me ragged! The link between the two groups is my incredible and beautiful wife, Jeanine, whose love continues to be a constant source of strength.

גם לאביאל

Preface

This book began its journey to fruition many years ago when I was a Lecturer at the Management School at Imperial College. At that time I was approached by Tony Moore and asked to contribute a textbook in Finance to the Imperial College Press. Early progress was swift, but soon slowed down due to the interference of "life's rich tapestry" as appears to often be the case. Having started the book as a single man with no major attachments (notwithstanding a passion for Tottenham Hotspur F.C.!), this book enters publication with the author a married man with two young children.

In writing this book I have been led by my own comments on texts from my student days, as well as by those of my own groups of students on the many contemporary texts in this area. One consequence is that I have tried to keep this book relatively short, to the point, and maintain a good flowing narrative. Too often, undergraduate textbooks drown the reader in a sea of numerous examples, so that the flow of the material gets lost and it becomes difficult to "see the wood for the trees". I have deliberately opted for a short, focused text, rather than the more encyclopædic variety that inhabits and weighs down too many student bookshelves. I have also tried to maintain a sense of high quality, readable English that treats the reader as an equal. I hope that I will be regarded as successful in these areas. As always, any errors, both of omission and commission, remain my own responsibility.

Acknowledgements

This book would never have come to fruition had it not been for the love and support of my wife, the "stupendously sexy" Jeanine. A debt of thanks is also due to my young children, David Jonathan ("Yoni") and Maya Isabella, who must have wondered what it was their father was doing at his G3 Macintosh computer on so many occasions. I am also indebted to my stepson, Aviel Levy, for his support and encouragement.

I would also like to record my thanks to my three brothers, Steven, Alan and Neil, as well as to their respective families, for their support, often in the form of familial banter.

This project began at the prompting of Tony Moore, then of Imperial College Press, and his help in getting the book started was invaluable. Since then I have benefited from the valuable insights of the Imperial College Press team.

A number of friends, colleagues and students were kind enough to read drafts and offer comments. My thanks go out in particular to Raymond Antian, Daniel Cohen (no relation), Catherine Dick, Sharon Foley, Debby McLean, and Mihail Nedev, although the responsibility for any errors remains squarely with me. At Imperial College Press, I am indebted to Geetha Nair and Gabriella Frescura for trying to ensure I made some kind of timely progress, as well as to Kim Tan for substantive comments on draft versions of the text. More recently I owe a huge debt of thanks to Katie Lydon for her editing prowess.

Finally, my thanks go out to the Spurs-List, an e-mail forum, which brought me and my wife together, as well as enabling me to be blessed with an abundance of great friends. I also would like to thank Tottenham Hotspur F.C., whom I have followed through thick and thin (mostly the latter in recent years!) as both man and boy. I hope this book finds as receptive an audience as the teams of Billy Nicholson, Keith Burkinshaw, and whomever is the manager when this book finally hits the shelves.

Contents

1.   Introducing Finance

The main objective of this book is to introduce and familiarise the reader with the financial management of the business enterprise. This involves learning the **language** of finance, the **environment** in which finance takes place, as well as a number of **methods** of financial analysis. Additionally, a number of finance theories are discussed on the basis that understanding them will enhance the ability to make financial decisions. Some of the theories have yet to find a consensus among financial economists, and thus there are several views that need to be considered.

While my aim is to make the subject matter "user friendly", there is a certain amount of technical material that cannot be avoided. Nonetheless, mathematical material has been kept to a discreet minimum, and even those with "mathematics-phobia" should be able to glean much more than the gist of the argument!

For many people the words finance and money are equivalent. However, such thinking can obscure the real insights that finance has to offer. While money is an object that enhances trade, finance is a field involved with decision-making concerning the use of money and credit; it is simultaneously an art and a science. Like all economic decision-making, finance involves a weighing-up of benefits against costs, and is therefore very much a sub-field of economics. Cost in economics refers to the concept of **opportunity cost:** "the cost of the next best alternative foregone". Thus, cost does not simply mean what has been paid for a given commodity, but rather what else might have been purchased instead. While in many cases both benefits and costs can be measured in monetary terms, this is not always possible, and there is increasing effort being made by finance experts to find methods to estimate or "proxy" non-monetary valuations. Costs and benefits for which no market valuation is available are often referred to as **externalities**. Their measurement or valuation is especially important for investments being undertaken by the public sector or those which are likely to have a significant social or environmental impact (which might be positive or negative).

It is important to think of finance as an economic phenomenon that occurs **in time**. For any economic agent—such as an individual, a business, or government—the timing of inflows of funds and outflows of funds will not automatically balance. Almost everyone who has been a student has had to experience the problem of bills needing to be paid when the grant (or loan) for the current period has run out. Finance might be thought of as the art of bringing fund inflows and outflows into some kind of balance. On these grounds finance may best be considered visually, occurring along a time-line:

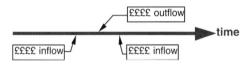

Visualisation of the flows of funds can also be made by proper use of a computer spreadsheet:

Time period	0	1	2	3	4
Cash inflows			£3,000	£5,000	£6,000
Cash outflows	(£10,000)	(£1,000)	(£500)	(£500)	(£500)
Net cash flow	(£10,000)	(£1,000)	£2,500	£4,500	£5,500

1.1   The Stuff of Finance

Ultimately, finance is about making decisions. **Personal finance** deals with making individual and family financial decisions: where to save, what type of insurance or pension scheme meets a person's requirements, and so on. This book focuses on **corporate finance**, which deals with financial decision-making within the context of the firm. The same principles we discuss apply equally to the not-for-profit firm. Other areas of finance might include investment management, or financial markets and institutions.

Although there may be an element of the abstract, financial theory aims to provide financial decision-makers with better tools. Better tools make for better decisions. Equally, finance can also help decision-makers understand better the environment within which they operate. A good financial manager needs both to understand the markets and institutions with which they are dealing, as well as the driving forces which bring about changes to the financial system.

While finance today is essentially a well-defined area, the subject matter has changed over time. It would not be an exaggeration to suggest that before the twentieth century finance was largely about the study of banking, and the relationship of the firm to its bank. The start of the twentieth century saw the beginning of a secular growth of other, non-bank financial intermediaries as well as an ever-increasing turnover and expansion of financial markets, and this brought about a change in perspective. For most of the first half of the twentieth century finance remained largely a descriptive, institutional subject, more the precinct of legal minds than economists. However, by the 1950s things had begun to change, and finance as we know it today was beginning to take shape.

From the work of Joel Dean [1951] real investment appraisal (**capital budgeting**, covered in Chapter Six) began to develop, and with it the use of mathematical techniques for financial analysis and decision-making. With the seminal work of Harry Markowitz [1952, 1958] on financial investment appraisal (**portfolio theory**, covered in Chapter Seven), the subject matter of finance really took off, becoming both more technical and more insightful. This is a trend which has continued up to the present day and seems likely to continue for the foreseeable future. This is especially so given the current vogue for establishing models for the pricing of derivatives. Those involved in constructing such models are often referred to as "rocket scientists", as they often come from a strongly numerate background in physics, for example. However, it is worth noting that it is often several years before developments in finance theory are taken up by practitioners. Thus, there are still areas of finance theory that have yet to be exploited in practice.

1.2   The Firm

1.2.1   What is a firm?

According to the dictionary, a firm may be defined as "a partnership for the undertaking of business" and also "the business itself". In common usage the words "firm", "business", "company", "organisation" and even "concern" are often used interchangably. The phrase "enterprise" is also used, but typically to imply an ambitious firm, perhaps with a (somewhat) cavalier attitude towards risk. For our purposes we need to be more rigorous, and define a firm on either a legal basis or on a functional or economic basis.

A firm might be regarded as a set of legal relationships between the various components (**stakeholders**) of which it is comprised. These relationships are typically expressed in contractual form, either explicitly or implicitly perhaps via custom. Thus, the firm will have a contractual relationship with its shareholders and another contractual relationship with its employees, whether thcy arc in a management role or labour. The firm has a relationship with its customers and suppliers, usually defined by the contractual terms of the sales invoice. Firms have contractual agreements with those who fund them by way of loans, embodied in the loan agreement. A firm also has a contractual relationship with the state: implicitly through abiding by the rule of law and more explicitly if the firm is a corporation (see Section 1.2.3). Multinational companies (MNCs) will have such relationships with several governments, depending on the countries in which the MNC operates.

The firm may be seen by way of its functions. This approach is often referred to as the firm being a "black box", in which inputs or resources are converted into outputs for sale:

Economists refer to the inputs as "factors of production". The primary factors are land (including extractive and natural resources), labour (of all kinds, including entrepreneurial), and capital (meaning **real capital**, or productive equipment, rather than **financial capital**). Increasingly, capital has come to include **human capital**, which encompasses human knowledge and the wisdom to employ that knowledge ("technology" in its broadest context).

This is diagrammatically equivalent to the economist's production function, which says that the level of output of a firm, q, is a function of the level of its inputs:

$$q = f(g, l, k)$$

where g = land, l = labour, and k = capital. The level of output, q, will form the firm's sales volume, with anything unsold going into inventory. Thus, q depends upon customer demand for the firm's products. The labour input, l, consists of the hours worked by labour and management, which in turn will be partly dependent upon their levels of remuneration. Given that labour is a significant stakeholder in the firm, the welfare (utility) of labour is significantly dependent upon the well-being of the firm. Additionally, labour remuneration often consists of a share options component, giving labour a shareholder stake in the firm.

The purchase of land and capital is funded from a mix of debt funding (e.g. from banks, bondholders, etc; see Chapter Four) and equity funding (from shareholders; see Chapter Five). Indeed, the value of the firm is the sum of its debt and equity funding:

$$V = B + S$$

where V = the value of the firm, B = the value of debt, and S = the value of equity. The immediate implication would seem to be that the value of the firm is independent of the mix of debt funding to equity funding. Whether or not this is the case is one of the issues we shall examine in Chapter Nine.

1.2.2   The objective of the firm

Microeconomists typically suggest that a firm tries to maximise its profits (subject to the costs imposed by the production function). However, the question remains as to whether pursuit of **profit**

maximisation would act to increase the well-being (welfare or utility) of the firm's owners, the shareholders. While it is true that different shareholders typically have different individual welfare preferences, if the management of the firm seeks to increase the value of shareholder wealth then that would act to increase the overall welfare of shareholders *in toto*. Thus, the true objective for the firm should be the maximisation of shareholder wealth. This would mean acting to maximise the value of the firm as measured by the price of each share.

1.1.2.1 Profit maximisation or wealth maximisation?

Economics textbooks which argue that the objective of the firm is to maximise profits are taking a simplified "single-period" view of the firm's operations. However, **value maximisation**—the maximisation of the value of the firm, or the maximisation of shareholder wealth—is a broader objective than profit maximisation. Indeed, value maximisation encompasses profit maximisation! For single-period analysis, the two methods are equivalent. For multi-period analysis, value maximisation is preferable.

Firstly, profits are essentially short-run. They are typically measured on an annual or semi-annual basis. While the accrual of profits serves to enhance the value of the firm, the maximisation of current profits may involve undertaking activities that actually jeopardise future profits. One example might be that of a firm improving its current profits by reducing maintenance spending on its capital equipment. This would very likely shorten the useful length of the equipment's lifetime, and mean a significant increase in future expenditure on capital; a case of "penny wise, pound foolish". To maximise value, the firm must take into account the long-run future stream of profits.

Secondly, profit maximisation fails to take into account **risk**. For example, in considering two possible investment projects, a firm operating under the goal of pure profit maximisation would undertake whichever project offered the highest expected future profits, even it that project meant having to take levels of risk that might be considered unacceptable. It might be the case that a lower-risk alternative offers a more robust, if smaller, level of profits, which is more acceptable to shareholders. As we shall see, value explicitly incorporates risk, so value maximisation takes account of risk in a way that profit maximisation does not.

In summary, value maximisation offers a sounder basis for decision-making than profit maximisation. It better describes the true objective of the firm, and provides a logical basis for optimal decision-making based on rigorous analytical procedures. Nonetheless, empirical evidence suggests that firms in the United Kingdom often adopt other objectives. A major postal questionnaire study of the financial objectives of 208 large UK firms was conducted in both 1980 and 1986 by R. H. Pike and T. S. Ooi [1988]. With a response rate from senior finance executives in excess of 70 per cent, and with 5 indicating "very important" and 1 "unimportant", their results can be summarised as follows:

Table 1: The Relative Importance of Financial Objectives

Objective	1980	1986
Short-term (1–3 years)		
Profitability	4.28	4.61
(e.g., percentage rate of return on investment)		
Profits or earnings (i.e., a profit target)	4.01	4.41
Long-term (3+ years)		
Growth in sales	3.18	2.97
Growth in earnings per share	2.83	4.38
Growth in shareholders' wealth	3.07	4.06

This shows quite clear evidence of a British penchant for "short-termism", although there appears to be a growing realisation of the importance of longer-term goals, indicated by the increasing importance attached to EPS growth and shareholders' wealth growth. It should also be noted that this evidence is quite consistent with results obtained from similar studies for both the United Kingdom and the United States.

1.3 Corporate Structure

1.3.1 Sole proprietorship

Once upon a time, the sole proprietorship (or **sole trader**) was known as the "one-man firm". Under this form of organisation, the firm *is* a single individual, and there is no legal distinction between the firm as an entity and the owner. That is to say, the firm has **unlimited liability**, and the assets of the owner can be called upon to meet the obligations of the firm. Because the firm is not a separate legal entity, it will not be subject to corporate taxation. However, the owner will be subject to personal income taxes on the firm's earnings, and the personal assets of the owner could be taken to pay off the firm's debts.

Because of its unlimited liability, it is unlikely that the sole proprietorship will be able to attract sizeable amounts of external funding. In part, this is due to the limited resources a sole proprietor typically has by way of collateral. It is often the case that as the business of the sole proprietorship grows, the owner will eventually seek to incorporate. Because the existence of the firm depends on the identity of its owner, the lifespan of the sole proprietorship depends on the lifespan of the owner.

Because a sole proprietorship means that the firm is the owner, there is a natural tendency to think of the firm as having no other employees. This is not necessarily the case, although in practice it quite often is.

1.3.2   Partnership

A partnership occurs whenever two or more persons associate for the purpose of conducting business. The partnership agreement may be oral or it may take a more formal basis. The profits of a partnership are taxed as personal income, usually on a *pro rata* basis. Not all partners need contribute financial resources; it is possible for some partners to be included because of the nature of the skills they bring to the venture. It is on this basis that some accountants and lawyers have established partnerships in the United Kingdom. Partners in such professions often work their way up through the ranks, and ultimately are rewarded by being made a partner in the company.

Nowadays, it is possible for some partners to be included in the partnership agreement with limited liability. However, under such a **limited partnership**, there still must be some general partners who have unlimited liability.

Under the partnership agreement, the partners share *pro rata* in the profits of the company. They are also both jointly and separately liable to make good any losses, and are personally liable for any debts the company incurs. The death or withdrawal of a partner, or a new partner coming into the business, results in the cessation of the existing partnership and the creation of a new one. For a partnership to work well, it is important to set up the partnership agreement to avoid potential conflicts. Terms and conditions for distribution of assets upon dissolution may be included in the agreement. One example is that it has become common practice for each partner to carry life assurance, with the other partners named as beneficiaries.

In February 1997, the British government proposed the introduction of **limited liability partnerships** (LLPs). These came into being on 6 April 2001 under the Limited Liability Partnerships Act 2000 and Regulations 2001. This legislation allowed for the creation of a new corporate entity with the flexibility of a partnership allied with limited liability status. An LLP provides the benefits of limited liability but allows its members the flexibility of organising their internal structure as a traditional partnership. The LLP is a separate legal entity and, while the LLP itself will be liable for the full extent of its assets, the liability of the members will be limited. Disclosure requirements for LLPs are similar to those of a company: financial information filed is equivalent to that of limited companies, including annual accounts.

1.3.3 Limited companies

A limited company (or **corporation**) is a separate legal entity from its owners and managers. Some would argue that a limited company is an "artificially created legal person". The owners of the corporation—known as **shareholders**—hold shares according to the proportion of the company they own. In the event of the company going bankrupt, any individual owner's liability is limited to their stake in the company as measured by the value of their shares. Personal assets may not be taken to pay off the company's debts; the company's liabilities are said to be limited.

The benefit of limited liability is that all profits and gains accrue to the shareholders. Any firm which is incorporated (i.e. has limited liability) is subject to corporate taxation. Shares in corporations are typically transferable from one individual to another.

Because a corporation does not depend on who its shareholders are, its lifespan can far exceed those of its shareholders. Indeed, the lifespan of a corporation may be considered indefinite. At each corporation's Annual General Meeting, the shareholders elect a Board of Directors (who might also be shareholders) to run the company on their behalf. As a company grows in size, the management of a corporation may become increasingly divorced from its ownership; i.e. the directors may choose to employ others ("managers") to administer the day-to-day affairs of the company. According to Companies House publication *CHN 15: Notes for Guidance: Directors and Companies House*,

> A director is appointed to manage the affairs of a company in accordance with its articles of association and the law generally. …

> Every company director has a personal responsibility to ensure that certain statutory documents are delivered to the Registrar of Companies as and when required by the Companies Act.

Failure to file documents such as accounts or annual returns with Companies House on time is a criminal offence, which can lead to a fine of up to £5,000, and ultimately the disqualification of a director.

Setting up a limited company in the United Kingdom is relatively straightforward, and can be done directly or via a Company Formation Agency. Most of the major Company Formations Agencies in the United Kingdom advertise in the weekly publication *Exchange and Mart*. However, individuals who have already been in business—perhaps as a sole proprietor—often incorporate using their accountants or lawyers as the formation agent. This is typically more costly, and in many cases the lawyer or accountant will simply employ a Company Formation Agency to do the work and add a margin on to the bill they send their client.

Directly or otherwise, application for incorporation is made to the Registrar of Companies, based at Companies House. Providing that the name of the firm is not already on The Register and that the proposed directors are not barred from being directors, the incorporation will be completed in about a week. A certificate of incorporation indicating the company number will be issued by Companies House. Documents known as the Memorandum and Articles of Association set out the rights and obligations of the firm. In essence, these form a contract between the corporation and the state. Corporations are required to file accounts annually with Companies House. All information held at Companies House is available to the general public, sometimes for a nominal fee, often free. This can be accessed via telephone, or by using the on-site computer terminals. Alternatively, an online service is offered, providing remote access to the Companies House system from a modem-linked personal computer. Available via the Internet at www.companieshouse.gov.uk, the site offers on-line registration, company searches, a list of disqualified directors, brochures and documentation and much more.

Similar arrangements for setting up a corporation exist in most countries. In the USA, where each state has its own laws, many businesses prefer to incorporate in Nevada or Delaware, where the regulatory burden is considered less onerous.

(Private) Limited Company

This refers to a corporation whose shares are not freely transferable. Shareholders may transfer (sell) their shares to a third party, but usually only with the express permission of the corporation. Private limited companies are required to use the phrase "**Limited**" or "**Ltd**" after the company name in all of their documentation. In the United States, the term "Inc." or "Incorporated" is used.

Public Limited Company (plc)

A public limited company is a corporation whose shares may be directly purchased from an existing shareholder without the permission of the company. Public limited companies are required to use the phrase "plc" after the company name in all of their documentation. Note that there is a distinction between **public limited companies** (plcs) and **listed companies**: while a listed company must be a plc, not all plcs are listed on the London Stock Exchange.

In order for a plc to become listed there are a number of requirements which it must first meet. Chief among these is the minimum capital requirement; it is unusual for a company with a capitalisation of less than £10 million to seek a listing. Additionally, for a company to gain a full listing in the stock exchange at least 25 per cent of its shares must be in public hands.

1.4   The Finance Function

The phrase **finance function** is often used to indicate that part of the firm concerned with the firm's financial affairs. The finance function may also be referred to as the financial department, or the firm's financial managers.

Given that the objective of the firm is to maximise the value of the firm (thereby maximising shareholder wealth), we can say that **the main function of financial management is to plan for, acquire, and utilise funds in such a way that shareholder wealth is maximised**. In order to fulfil such a role, the financial manager must have a keen knowledge and sound understanding of both the firm and the financial system. This can be summarised in the following diagram:

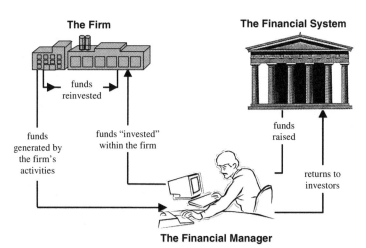

Particularly in larger firms, the functions of the Financial Manager (Financial Director or **CFO**—Chief Financial Officer) are often divided into (at least) two major areas of responsibility:

Treasurer   Responsible for the acquisition and custody of funds

Controller   Responsible for accounting, reporting and control

Additionally, the Control function is often sub-divided to include a separate function with responsibility for taxation issues, which have a particularly significant impact on firms operating across national boundaries. This division can best be understood diagrammatically:

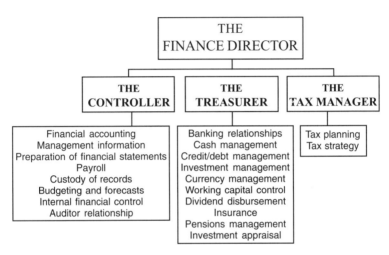

1.5   Principals and Agents

In the early days of the industrial revolution, the firm was usually managed by those who owned it, much like the small family-run business of today. Because the modern corporation tends to be a large, complex organisation, a divorce has arisen between those who own the firm (shareholders) and those who run it (managers, typically the Board of Directors). In the modern corporation, it is the task of management—the **agents**—to administer the firm on behalf of its owners—the **principals**. This is known as an **agency relationship**. In the past, it was often assumed that there was no divergence of interests between the firm's owners and managers, but increasingly this does not seem to be the case. A conflict of interest between those who own the firm and those who manage it appears to be the norm rather than the exception. There is a tendency for managers to make decisions that may be in their own interest but not in the interest of shareholders or consistent with the risks bondholders accepted when they purchased their stake in the company.

Such conflicts give rise to additional costs, known as **agency costs**. These costs, which are not easily measured in monetary terms, represent opportunities which have been foregone as a result. For example, while management might consider a corporate aircraft useful, it might not be in the shareholders' interest. One way of minimising these costs is to turn agents into principals. This can occur when the directors of a company are also shareholders (a primary aim of the use of employee share options). There are four key areas of agency cost:

- Costs of minimising the incentives for management to act contrary to the interests of shareholders
- Costs of monitoring the actions of management
- Bonding costs to protect shareholders from managerial dishonesty
- Opportunity costs of lost profits due to complex organisational structures, which limit managerial decision-making flexibility

Further, there may be a conflict of interest between the firm's managers and its labour force. Thus within the firm's operations there may be a three-way conflict of interest. Further conflicts of interest may arise as a result of the firm's sources of financing. Investors can provide funds to a firm via debt or via equity. Bondholders—a shorthand term including any providers of debt to the firm—are likely to be affected in a different way by the firm's decisions than shareholders, leading to a conflict of interest between these groups. The key area of conflict concerns the appetite of these groups for risk. Because shareholders wish to see their wealth maximised *ceteris paribus* (other things being equal), they would prefer management to leverage their returns via prudent risk-taking. Alternatively, bondholders are primarily interested in the company doing enough to ensure that they receive their payments of interest (and repayment of principal in the longer run), which may involve a lower risk strategy. It may also be the case that conflicts of interest occur between groups of shareholders, or between groups of bondholders.

In recent years, an expanding body of literature has developed, investigating the various issues pertaining to conflicts of interest between a firm's various constituents or **stakeholders**. The seminal work in this area is probably the 1976 paper by M. C. Jensen and W. H. Meckling, which gave rise to the distinction between **maximising** behaviour and **satisficing** behaviour: the former indicating behaviour with the objective of maximising the value of the firm (or shareholder wealth), the latter indicating behaviour whereby management does "just enough" to keep shareholders content.

1.5.1   Maximising versus satisficing

Economic theory is built on the assumption that individuals are rational maximisers. The usual objective is for individuals to act to maximise their well-being subject to the constraints which are imposed by limited wealth or income. Economists typically use the concept of **utility** as a measure of an individual's well-being or welfare. Utility is largely a subjective measure: the individual decides what is in their best self-interest. However, this does not mean that individuals act in a purely selfish manner; there is a vast difference between acting in one's own interest and acting selfishly. It may well be in an individual's self-interest to donate funds to charity, or to consider how their actions impinge on others above their own immediate requirements. Self-interest usually includes the notion that most individuals prefer less risk to more, *ceteris paribus*; that is to say, individuals are normally **risk-averse**. Self-interest also implies that an individual prefers to receive a given sum of money now rather than in the future, *ceteris paribus*.

Maximising involves optimisation of a given objective: it implies striving for the best possible outcome. On the other hand, satisficing behaviour involves a willingness to settle for less than the best possible outcome. Jensen and Meckling established that a manager with fractional ownership (including zero ownership) might become inclined to adopt satisficing behaviour, rather than seeking to maximise the wealth of all shareholders. This imposes an agency cost on the shareholders. The increasing use of perquisites (perks) is sometimes cited as a symptom of satisficing behaviour. Increasingly shareholders are trying to structure the remuneration of directors to ensure maximising rather than satisficing behaviour.

1.5.2   Management goals

In the modern corporation, managers are employed to act on behalf of the shareholders. It has been argued, however, that managers may substitute their own goals in place of the objectives of the shareholders, who wish to see their own wealth maximised. As well as perks, managers may seek to pay themselves large salaries and other forms of remuneration—such as pensions and share options—regardless of the performance of the company. Recent publicity has highlighted strong shareholder concern about directors' remuneration, an issue often referred to in the press as "fat cats' pay". In the United Kingdom, this issue is occasionally highlighted by "shareholder revolts" at company AGMs. In some cases, the revolts have been brought about by larger, institutional investors, while in others groups of individual, small shareholders have been moved to actively voice their concerns. In the United Kingdom in 1995, the Greenbury Committee—chaired by Sir Richard Greenbury, chairman of Marks and Spencer—published a code of conduct on executive pay for corporations. A study carried out by PIRC, the corporate governance consultancy, suggested that in 1996 many companies were still in contravention of the Greenbury guidelines, especially in respect of the length of directors' contracts and long-term investment plans (L-tips). The issue of corporate governance is one which continues to test the minds and imaginations of both regulators and the regulated, yet the solution seems never to get closer. A case of two steps forward, one step backwards, and *vice versa* on occasion!

Managers may also have an agenda of "empire building", whereby they try to enhance their status through promotion or the pursuit of "status goals" such as the numbers of staff or the size of budget for which they are responsible. Because these goals focus only on part of the firm's operation, they may be inconsistent with the goal of shareholder wealth maximisation.

Finally, because managers depend on their position for their livelihood, they might well take a satisficing, more risk-averse view of the company's activities than would suit the shareholders. Shareholders have the option of diversifying away some of their risk by holding a portfolio of shares in different companies (see Chapter Seven).

1.5.3 Shareholders' goals

The main aim of any shareholder is to promote his or her individual well-being, usually in terms of the wealth that accrues. For shareholders, this increased wealth can take the form of income by way of dividends, and also capital gains through increases in the price of the shares. Capital gains may be **realised** (when the shares are actually sold) or unrealised, in which case they are "paper increases" in the shareholder's wealth. Capital gains can also be negative, when they then become known as capital losses.

Depending upon their individual preferences, some shareholders will seek to maximise their wealth through capital gains, while others may be more interested in the stream of dividend payments that a company offers. Institutional investors, such as pension funds and insurance companies, are a prime example of the latter, using the regular dividends they receive to meet their outgoings, such as pension payments. Investors who seek to make capital gains in the short-term from newly-issued shares are referred to as "stags". Issues of shares in the newly-privatised utilities during the 1980s were often offered at bargain-basement prices, leading to a great deal of successful stagging activity.

Whether investors are interested in capital gains or dividends, these can only arise ultimately from a company being successful (profitable) in the longer-run. That is to say, the interests of shareholders can be met only if the company is successfully adding value. Because this requires the investor to take a view on what the future holds for the company, it is considered to be speculative activity. It therefore requires a higher degree of risk-aversion on the part of the investor than if they were to hold bonds, for example.

1.5.4 Bondholders' goals

Although the term "debtholder" would be more appropriate and certainly more accurate, "bondholder" is the traditional term for any entity which has lent funds to the firm, regardless of whether or not bonds (marketable or otherwise) have been issued. Thus, a bank which has extended a loan to a firm would come under this classification.

By their very nature, bondholders are more risk averse than shareholders. Bondholders have usually opted for a certain return by way of regular interest payments on the funds they have lent to the firm. Shareholders have opted for the greater uncertainty of dividends and/or possible capital gains. It therefore follows that bondholders will typically prefer the firm to undertake less risky investments than would be preferred by shareholders.

1.5.5   Other stakeholders' goals

In addition to those who have a capital stake in the company, by way of debt or equity, there is a broader group of stakeholders whose activities directly affect the successful running of the firm. It may well be the case that the goals of these other stakeholders conflict with those of the shareholders, in whose interest the firm is supposed to be run. Additionally, there are stakeholders with a more tenuous connection to the company, but who still have an interest in its well-being. In no particular order, these other stakeholders include:

customers: without whom the company has no *raison d'être*. There is a direct connection between a company that can successfully offer customers the products they desire over time, and one that successfully achieves value maximisation.

workers: those who are employed to undertake the actual work of production within a company. History is replete with examples of conflicts between the workforce and the management of a company. However, it also needs to be noted that management are also part of the company's workforce.

suppliers: for a company to operate successfully it requires stability from its suppliers, in terms of price and quality of product, ability to deliver, and the supplier's existence. Suppliers include those who provide such necessities as raw materials (to a manufacturer, for example) and distributors, as well as those who provide indispensable services to the firm. These would include the company's accountants, any legal services required, as well as those who offer peripheral services such as local caterers offering lunch facilities.

the local community: firms have to operate within the local community, and to abide by local culture, customs, and taxation. Local infrastructure, such as transportation, is required for a firm's labour force to be able to get to and from work, and for the firm to be able to take delivery of raw materials and deliver its products to the customer.

government: the (national) government provides infrastructure and the laws within which firms operate. Firms have to operate within national laws of contract and other legal property rights, as well as having to comply with the laws on taxation.

society "at large": increasingly society places pressures on the way in which firms operate, through changing acceptable public standards (on the environment, for example), or via pressure groups, which seem to play an ever-increasing role in changing societal norms and standards.

1.5.6   In summary
All of the above suggests that, in the real world, managers may not operate in the best interests of shareholders. However, this is not to say that shareholders are powerless. There are a number of devices which can be utilised by shareholders to ensure that management comply with pursuit of the goals of shareholders:

directors: because the board of directors are elected by the shareholders, they can be terminated if the latter are dissatisfied with their performance. However, experience suggests that this is more likely in theory than in practice.

contracts: judicial arrangements for compensation and remuneration to management can be written into their contracts. Increasingly, use is made of performance-related measures, such as share options.

takeovers: if a firm is considered to be sound with the exception of its management, it is liable to be considered ripe for a takeover bid.

In the event of a takeover, the existing management would be sacked and replaced. Thus, the fear of takeover acts as an incentive for managers to pursue actions which will positively impact the share price, thereby maximising shareholder wealth.

labour market competition: this works in a similar yet localised way to the fear of takeover, and has been used by well-paid managers as an explanation of their compensation packages. Put simply, there is a labour market for management, in the same way as there is a market for any other form of labour. Poor managers will be readily replaced by better managers. Those firms willing to pay the most will be able to attract the best management. That there is a global market for top management is one of the arguments put forward (in the United Kingdom) to justify large executive compensation packages. Nonetheless, there is some evidence to suggest that there is some degree of segmentation of national markets for executives. Thus, while the argument for market competition seems to hold for a very large economy like the United States, the evidence for the United Kingdom seems to be more questionable.

1.6   Finance versus Accounting

To many people the terms "accounting" and "finance" are synonymous. Although there is a strong symbiosis, there is a distinct difference between these two fields. Nonetheless, in smaller firms, the functions of "finance" and "accounting" may well both be performed by the same person or group of people. To some degree one could argue that "finance" is what is performed by the **treasury** function, and "accounting" is performed by the **control** function, based on the diagram on page 13. There is strong anecdotal evidence suggesting that accountants tend to over emphasise the closeness between accounting and finance, while financial economists tend to emphasise the distinction. This can be seen at first hand when observing the appointments columns for financial positions, which in the United Kingdom are largely advertisements for qualified accountants. In larger firms where there is increasingly a division of labour within the finance function, this might not be a good thing given the divergence of the skill-sets between finance professionals and accountants.

Primarily, accounting is responsible for financial record-keeping, and hence the provision of information by which sound financial decisions can be made. Thus, accounting offers both a stewardship and accountability function. Accounting is the means by which records of the firm's financial activities are recorded and audited to ensure that the best possible (legitimate) use is made of the firm's resources. One major way this is done is via the production of financial reports—"the accounts". According to the United Kingdom's Accounting Standards Committee [1975], the object of these financial reports is

> ... to communicate economic measurements of, and information about resources and performance of the reporting entity useful to those having reasonable rights to such information.

Thus, financial reports are one means by which the principals—shareholders—can check on the actions of their agents—the management. They also allow debt-holders and other stakeholders, as well as various analysts, to gain some insight into what the firm has been doing. The accounts are also the basis on which the firm is subject to taxation.

Finance, on the other hand, refers to the making of financial decisions. If financial managers are to make sound decisions, they require the best possible (financial and other) information. Thus, finance may be seen as a decision-making structure built on the foundations of sound accounting. Indeed, the past is really the only true guide we have to the future, however imperfect. Nonetheless, because the kind of information contained within financial reports is primarily for reporting purposes, it is not necessarily the same kind of information that financial managers require for making decisions.

For example, financial accounts are normally prepared on an accruals basis. For valuations to be calculated, finance requires cash flows. Earnings per share and cash flow per share are not the same thing, as the former will typically include monies which have yet to flow into or out of the firm. Indeed, it is possible to find a company which appears profitable but is in fact suffering from negative cash flows.

There is also the question of "window dressing" or "creative accounting". By adopting certain types of accounting policies, firms try to give the impression that their business is in better shape than it is in reality to maintain investor confidence; sometimes they try to make the firm appear worse off to avoid paying taxes! Profits—the "bottom line"—are derived based on a series of assumptions, usually those provided by the Accounting Standards Committee, and increasingly the standards laid down by the London-based International Accounting Standards Committee (IASC). Nonetheless, there remains much inconsistency, to the extent that some cynics still argue that corporate accounts are largely a work of fiction. Providing a company adopts a consistent policy for accounting, it is possible to compare its year-on-year performance, although comparison with other firms (who may have different accounting policies) may be spurious.

We now move on to consider in greater detail the various issues we have addressed in this chapter. Remember, however, that the journey is at least as important as the destination.

2.   The Financial Environment

Anyone considering a venture into Finance—for either practical or academic reasons—is best advised to have a sound knowledge of the financial environment. The finance function (financial manager) of the firm needs to be knowledgeable about the workings and state of the financial system, because it is from this sector that funds will be raised, and to which funds ultimately need to be repaid. Because the financial sector is a crucial component of the wider macroeconomy we begin our survey by considering this connection.

2.1   Macroeconomics and Finance

Although it is rarely demonstrated, there is a strong relationship between the subject matter of macroeconomics and that of finance. This relationship is most clearly seen via the Circular Flow of Income diagram which has become a standard in most macroeconomics texts:

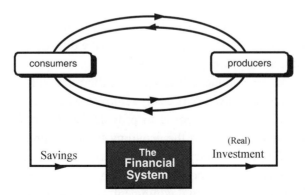

This standard diagram clearly shows that the role of the financial system is to channel funds from savers to productive investments. In this context, savers are often referred to as "surplus units" (they have more current income available than they immediately require), while investors are referred to as "deficit units" (they have less current income available than they immediately require). Because the financial system acts as a conduit to channel funds from surplus units to deficit units, it acts to (i) provide an increased incentive for saving to take place, and (ii) encourage and facilitate investment. If investment is higher than would otherwise be the case, then economic activity (typically measured by GDP, Gross Domestic Product) is likely to be higher in direct consequence.

2.2   The Financial System: Markets and Institutions

The financial system remains one of the least understood aspects of the world in which we live; to many its mystery is both magical and foreboding. The sums of money discussed are so large that they often resemble international telephone numbers, and the crises and scandals that occur do little to reassure us of the integrity of those who work within the financial system. And yet the financial system is a crucial component of the modern macroeconomy, with which we all come into daily contact.

Much of the mystery surrounding the financial system arises because it operates on both a retail and a wholesale basis. However, most of us are only exposed to the retail side: the retail (or high street) banks, building societies, and, less frequently, insurance companies and pension funds. Indeed, only a small proportion of us have direct experience of the retail side of trading in company shares.

In terms of the volume of transactions, the retail side is very much the lesser aspect. The mystery is easily removed when one considers that the role of the financial system is to provide for the transfer of funds from surplus units (savers) in the economy to deficit units (borrowers). This is true for any country, and throughout all periods of history. Historically most of the borrowing has been undertaken by firms, enabling the purchase of capital equipment, often on a large scale. Such capital equipment tends to act as an engine of economic growth both directly—because workers need to be employed in its manufacture—and indirectly—it enables firms to produce their products more efficiently and profitably. Without the financial system, firms would have to fund all of their capital purchases from their own reserves, making investment much less likely to occur.

The foundation which underpins the financial system is money. Money is the financial core which enables us to perform our daily transactions. It also offers a medium by which we can postpone transactions: we can sell something now for money, and retain that money for a transaction in the future. This is not the case with a barter transaction. Around this monetary core, there are the three pillars which allow the financial system to function:

1. **The various financial institutions**: banks and building societies, insurance companies and pension funds, and the various investment trusts and unit trusts.

2. **The financial markets**: the stock exchange, where both shares and debt instruments are issued ("primary market") and traded ("secondary market"), the foreign exchange markets, and the increasingly topical derivatives markets.

3. **The regulators**: in most financial systems, the financial markets and institutions are subject to constraints on their activities imposed by the regulatory regime. This may consist of self-regulatory organisations, or regulatory agencies set up by the government, or some combination of both.

Both the financial institutions and the financial markets serve as conduits for channelling funds from savers to investors. In our everyday lives, we see many of the retail aspects of the institutions, but for many, direct experience of the markets is much more limited. The same may be said for firms: larger firms are likely to have greater, more direct experience of all aspects of the financial system than are smaller firms. It is unlikely, for example, that the owner of a small fruit stall in a street market will try to raise funds via a share flotation on the stock exchange! However, virtually all firms of every size will have arranged an overdraft facility (or line of credit) with their bank.

In addition to the usual laws pertaining to property rights and contracts, most financial systems are subject to regulation. There may be several objectives of the regulation: to ensure the soundness and stability of the financial system, and therefore maintain confidence in it; to ensure consumer protection; to prevent any build-up of monopoly power; and so on. In theory, regulatory bodies can be external to the system, such as a government agency, or internal, known in the United Kingdom as a self-regulatory organisation (SRO). It is often the case that the banking system is regulated by the central bank, which is also responsible for the conduct of monetary policy. In some countries the central bank operates as an agency of the government, while increasingly in the higher income economies the central bank operates independently of government, although the key central bankers are typically appointed by government. In the UK, following the election of the Labour government in 1997, the Bank of England was granted "operational independence". This meant that the Bank of England no longer operated monetary policy as a branch of central government, but did so independently within the inflation guidelines established by the government via legislation.

The key legislative act which established the current financial regulation regime in the United Kingdom is the Financial Services and Markets Act (2000). This Act set up the Financial Services Authority (FSA) a specialised regulatory body for policing large parts of "the City", as the financial district of London is known. Full details can be found on the government's website at www.hmso.gov.uk/acts/acts2000/20000008.htm.

2.2.1   Types of financial market

In practice, there are various kinds of financial market, typically based on the type of financial asset which is being traded. The financial manager needs to be familiar with both the panoply of markets and the language of those markets. One basic distinction is that between the debt markets and the equity market. In the former, securities which represent corporate debt obligations ("bonds") are traded; in the latter, equity securities such as ordinary shares (known as "common stock" in the United States) are traded. Bonds and equity are discussed in detail in Chapters Four and Five respectively.

Another distinction is made between "money markets" and "capital markets". The distinction is one based on the time to maturity of the assets being traded. Thus, money markets are those in which financial instruments with a maturity of less than one year are traded. Capital markets are those in which instruments with a maturity of more than one year are traded. Because equity has a (potentially) infinite lifespan, the money markets are exclusively debt markets by definition, whereas the capital markets include both debt (medium-term and long-term) markets and equity markets.

Financial markets also distinguish between primary markets and secondary markets. **Primary** markets are those in which securities are traded for the first time, such as when a company's shares are first floated. **Secondary** markets refer to those in which previously-issued securities are traded. Thus, it is in the primary markets that firms raise funds; the secondary markets provide for liquidity by allowing the transfer of ownership of securities.

In addition, there may also be markets for derivative securities. Such derivatives are securities which have no intrinsic value of their own. Rather they derive their value from that of some underlying asset, which is usually a financial asset (such as the ordinary shares in a company, or interest rates) or a real asset or commodity (such as gold, silver, oil, etc.). The underlying assets are said to trade in a "cash market". Following a series of mergers down the years, LIFFE (the London International Financial Futures Exchange; now euronext•LIFFE) became the main market for derivatives in the United Kingdom. The largest and oldest derivatives markets are at the Chicago Mercantile Exchange (CME), and the Chicago Board of Trade (CBoT).

The primary purpose for which derivatives were designed is the hedging of risk. However, many derivatives are leveraged instruments; that is to say, a relatively small down-payment offers a disproportionately large exposure to price movements in the cash markets. This down-payment is known as a "margin" in the futures market, and as a "premium" for options transactions. Such leverage allows for hedging, but also for highly speculative behaviour. Indeed, it is because of speculative activity that went severely awry that derivatives have become well-known. Before the tragic disasters at Barings, Orange

County, Procter and Gamble, and Metallgeselleschaft, derivatives were largely an arcane subject for professionals, unheard of by the general public.

Derivatives fall into three basic categories: futures, options, and swaps:

Futures are standardised forward contracts. In its simplest form this means one counterparty is implicitly paying an agreed price now for the future delivery of a commodity, which will have a standardised quality, a standardised quantity, and a standardised delivery date. Futures contracts may be "financial" or "commodity". Examples of financial futures include interest rate futures, exchange rate futures, and stock index futures. Commodity futures include both "soft" commodities such as foodstuffs (including such esoterica as orange juice futures and pork belly futures), and "hard" commodities such as metals and oil. Futures markets operate through a central clearing house, which guarantees the trade to both counterparties.

Options are derivatives which offer the right (but not the obligation) to buy or sell the underlying asset at a guaranteed price on or before the expiration date. An option to buy is called a "call option"; an option to sell is called a "put option". The price paid for an option is called the "option premium" and is typically a small fraction of the market price of the underlying asset. The price paid to exercise the option (that is, to buy or sell the underlying asset) is called the "strike price" or "exercise price". Options come in two basic "flavours": "American" options allow the option to be exercised any time up to and including the date of expiration; "European" options can only be exercised on the expiration date.

The largest single category of options tends to be equity options, which are usually standardised and therefore tradable in the markets. However, less standardised, over-the-counter (OTC) options are feasible, if not entirely marketable.

Swaps refer to an exchange of payments, but because these tend to be unstandardised, there is typically no market as such in which they can be traded. Thus they are considered to be over-the-counter (OTC) transactions.

2.2.2 Efficient markets

At its most general, efficiency means getting the most output for the least inputs. In a sense, efficiency is effective laziness. The output of a market is the quantity of products it trades; the input is measured by the cost of swiftly transferring the product from suppliers to purchasers. Thus, in general a market can be said to be efficient if the largest possible quantity of products is traded quickly at the lowest possible cost. For a financial market, the product is funds or financial capital.

Because in a market the price will adjust to reflect the activities of buyers and sellers, it may be said that in an efficient market the price will adjust swiftly to fully reflect the information available to buyers and sellers on which they base their activities. Any profits which can be made on the basis of existing information will already have been realised; that is to say, that profitable opportunities will be "arbitraged" out. In an efficient market it is not possible to earn superior returns to the market consistently, except by pure chance.

One key implication of this is that if a market is efficient then all information is said to be discounted already (that is, reflected in the price), and no excess (risk-adjusted) returns can be made except as the result of actions based on new information. The key here is the nature of the information being used to make decisions by capital market participants. It would make intuitive sense for information about (listed) companies to be considered relevant. It would also make sense for investors to be concerned with key macroeconomic indicators, such as inflation and GDP, as well as government policy designed to influence such variables. It would seem to make less sense to consider the weather (for example) as a factor influencing capital market returns. Nonetheless, the notion that the economy is affected by weather, which is in turn due to sunspot activity, has a long legacy dating back to William Stanley Jevons (1835–1882). More recent studies have begun to link economic activity with the threats of disease (AIDS, SARS) and terrorism. More fanciful notions include the positing of relations between overall market returns and key national sporting events (how the England national soccer team performs, for example, or the results of the Super Bowl in American football), as well as the "hemline" theory, which argues that stock market returns are related to the length of women's hemlines on their skirts! Based on the unpublished work of Harry Roberts [1967], economists make the case that there are three levels of efficiency for capital markets, based on the nature of the information set:

Weak-form efficiency

The lowest degree of market efficiency is such that current security prices fully reflect historical information on prices or rates of return. If a market is characterised by weak-form efficiency, then no investor can earn excess returns by using a strategy based on historical information. The implication is that past prices (returns) are a poor indicator of future prices (returns). Past trends or cycles do not act to predict future trends or cycles. There is a large body of empirical literature that offers evidence to suggest that capital markets in the developed world are at least weak-form efficient.

Semi-strong-form efficiency

The middle level goes beyond the use of historical data, to suggest that a market is semi-strong-form efficient if current security prices fully reflect all publicly available knowledge. Thus, in addition to historical data, various kinds of public announcement—changes in macroeconomic policy, corporate policy changes that affect the firm's cash flows, takeover announcements—will be swiftly incorporated into the price (return) on securities. It will not be possible to earn excess returns on the basis of publicly available information, as it will already have been discounted. Despite the occasional counterexample, there is strong empirical evidence that this form of market efficiency exists in capital markets with high volume and liquidity, such as those in the United Kingdom, the United States, Japan, Canada, and most of western Europe.

Strong-form efficiency

Strong-form efficiency implies that current security prices fully reflect all available information, whether publicly available or not. Under strong-form efficiency it is impossible to make excess returns by "insider dealing", that is to say, by trading on the basis of private information. The existence of insider trading regulations, and the high profile of insider dealing court cases, especially in the United States, strongly suggest that strong-form efficiency does not exist.

The relationship between the degree of efficiency of a financial market and the information set can be depicted graphically:

less information   more information

———▶

Weak-form efficiency	*Semi-strong-form efficiency*	*Strong-form efficiency*
Share prices reflect historical price and volume information	Share prices reflect all publicly available information	Share prices reflect all public and private information

One implication of this is that if markets are efficient, then no trend in prices will be discernible. Primarily this is because prices adjust swiftly to reflect new information, and new information becomes known in a random fashion. Thus, prices in an efficient market will follow a "random walk". The notion of a random walk, however, has its origins in empirical work: in a paper presented to the Royal Statistical Society in 1953, the statistician Maurice Kendall examined the behaviour of share and commodity prices to try and find cyclical patterns, and was surprised when he could not find any. In fact, this should have come as little surprise as his results had been anticipated in the doctoral work of Louis Bachelier [1900]. In addition, the random nature of commodity prices had been noted during the 1930s by Working, a food economist [1934]. From the corporate perspective, the key implication focuses directly on the objective of the firm: value maximisation. If capital markets are efficient, then share prices will be an unbiased estimate of the value of the firm.

2.3   Investment and Finance

Investment refers to a process whereby funds are paid out now in the expectation of enhanced future cash flows. Investment is embodied in time. **Real investment** occurs when a corporation pays out funds for the use of capital equipment, with which it expects to increase its value by enhancing its future profit stream. **Financial investment** occurs when the funds are supplied to a corporation in the expectation of future dividends (equity investment), future interest payments (loans), as well as a possible capital gain on the security which represents the financial investment. From the macroeconomic viewpoint, financial investment is really an act of saving, as we saw in the Circular Flow of Income diagram. It is the financial system that converts acts of financial investment into acts of real investment. In other words, it is the financial system that channels the funding which allows real investment to take place.

In the same way as there is a separation between the savings and (real) investment decisions within the macroeconomy, there is also the need for a separation of the investment and financing decisions within any firm. In Chapter Six we examine in detail the process by which prospective (real) investments are judged, in terms of their contribution to the firm's objective of maximising value. However, it is important to recognise that there are two distinct stages to this process. Firstly, any investment must be judged on its contribution to adding value to the firm in its own right. Secondly, the investment needs to be judged on the basis of how it is to be financed. In Chapters Eight and Nine we shall come across the (theoretical) proposition that how investments are financed is irrelevant to the investment decision. However, it is conceivable for an investment to be unprofitable *per se*, yet appear to be profitable once financing considerations have been taken into account. In such a case, the firm would be better off ignoring the investment project itself, and simply making profits by buying and selling financial claims (borrowing and lending) as it is the funding which is adding value. Theoretical underpinnings for this separation are to be found in Hirshleifer [1958], which built upon the earlier work of Fisher [1930].

2.4   Accounting for Finance

In order to be able to make sound financial decisions, the financial manager needs to be able to read the financial records of the company. Equally, investors may wish to examine the financial records of companies in which they are considering placing their monies. However, the financial records of a company are largely a matter of history which, while imperfect, offer our only guide to the company's future. Such "matters of history" for all United Kingdom companies with limited liability can be obtained from the records at Companies House. While the database of companies is computerised, company reports and accounts obtained via a "company search" (for which a small fee is involved) come in the form of a microfiche, which requires a microfiche reader. There are publicly available readers at Companies House, which include the facility to print selected pages from the microfiche to paper.

The financial records of a company are contained in its accounts or financial statements. These come in three basic forms, which firms trading as limited companies in the United Kingdom are required to publish:

- the balance sheet
- the income statement (or profit and loss statement), and
- the cash flow statement

Companies present these to shareholders, prospective shareholders and other interested parties in the form of their Annual Report and Accounts. The Annual Report also contains a statement from the Chairman of the Board of Directors as well as a listing of the directors, plus a note from the company's auditors verifying that the accounts are a "true and fair view of the state of affairs of the company", "free from material misstatement". For smaller firms Annual Reports tend to be little more than a basic attempt to meet legal requirements. However, larger firms, especially those with stock exchange listings, often produce glossy brochures that go beyond the legal requirements, appearing to be more the product of the company's marketing department than its accounting department. The required financial statements normally present little more than an overview, and are supplemented by more detailed "notes to the accounts". Obviously, firms in different industries are likely to have different items appearing in their financial statements. This makes it difficult on occasion to compare and contrast firms. It is also the case that firms within the same industry may have different accounting policies, again making it difficult to compare them via their financial statements.

2.4.1 The balance sheet

The balance sheet represents a snapshot picture of the firm's financial position at a given point in time. It is typically divided into two columns, showing the firm's assets in one, and the claims on its assets in the other. In the USA, the columns are depicted in terms of decreasing liquidity, with more liquid assets towards the top. While historically this has not been the case in the United Kingdom, accounting standards and conventions have been increasingly approaching those of the USA. "Current assets" are those which are expected to be converted to cash within a year. Less liquid assets—such as plant and equipment—are not expected to be converted to cash within a year and are referred to as "fixed assets". Similarly for claims on assets: current liabilities refer to those which must be met within a year. One example of a UK company balance sheet is presented below. Note that figures are presented both for the current year and the previous year.

Balance sheets
as at 31st May current year

	Note	current year £'000	previous year £'000
Fixed assets			
Intangible assets	11	15,816	10,901
Tangible assets	12	34,025	24,249
Investments	13	—	—
		49,841	35,150
Current assets			
Properties for resale		—	225
Stocks		188	263
Debtors	14	2,312	1,884
		2,500	2,372
Creditors:			
Amounts falling due within one year	15	(15,077)	(11,243)
Net current liabilities		(12,577)	(8,871)
Total assets less current liabilities		37,264	26,279
Creditors:			
Amounts falling due after more than one year	16	(9,949)	(3,393)
Net assets		27,315	22,886
Capital and reserves:			
Called up share capital	18	4,005	4,005
Share premium account	19	1,192	1,192
Revaluation reserve	19	2,916	2,969
Profit and loss account	19	19,202	14,720
Equity shareholders' funds		27,315	22,886

The financial statements were approved by the board of directors on 20th September current year.

Signed on behalf of the board
XXXXX
yyyyy   } Directors

2.4.2   The income statement

More traditionally known in the United Kingdom as a Profit and Loss account (or "P & L"), the income statement shows the results of various events which have impacted a firm over a given period of time. As with the balance sheet, both current date and the previous year are stated. If the balance sheet is analogous to a photograph, the income statement is a movie or video. Everything in this account stems from the revenues the company generates from its sales, i.e. **turnover**. Because profits are the difference between a firm's revenues and its costs, the costs of production, distribution, and (perhaps) financing costs are deducted from turnover to derive a figure for profits. Below we present the profit and loss account for the same firm whose balance sheet we considered previously:

Consolidated profit and loss account					
Year ended 31st May current year					
		current year		*previous year*	
	Note	**£'000**	**£'000**	*£'000*	*£'000*
Turnover – continuing operations	2		**25,083**		*22,326*
Cost of sales and distributions costs			**2,776**		*3,089*
Player and match expenses			**11,839**		*12,197*
Administrative expenses			**4,486**		*5,903*
			19,101		*21,189*
Operating profit – continuing operations	5		**5,982**		*1,137*
Net interest payable	4		**(629)**		*(252)*
Profit on ordinary activities before taxation			**5,353**		*885*
Taxation charge on profit on ordinary activities	6		**(443)**		*(288)*
			4,910		*597*
Profit on ordinary activities after taxation					
Dividends — declared	7	**(481)**		*(160)*	
— less waived		**—**		*85*	
			(481)		*(75)*
Retained profit for the financial year	9		**4,429**		*522*
Earnings per share	10		**30.7p**		*3.7p*

Statement of total recognised gains and losses		
	current year	*previous year*
	£'000	*£'000*
Profit for the financial year	**4,910**	*597*
Unrealised deficit on revaluation of freehold land and buildings	**—**	*(164)*
Total unrecognised gains and losses relating to the financial year	**4,910**	*433*

Movements on reserves are shown in note xy to the financial statements.

The notes on pages xx to zz form part of these financial statements.

2.4.3 The cash flow statement

The nature of accrual accounting is such that, for any given accounting period, funds paid out by way of expenses and those received for goods sold may not relate to the same items. For example, a company may be purchasing raw materials to use in its production process, yet not paying for them for some months due to trade credit conditions. It also happens that firms sell goods (or services) but do not receive payment for some time due to credit arrangements. Therefore, the profit and loss account may not accurately reflect the actual flow of cash into and out of a company's coffers. It is also the case that there may be non-cash items (such as depreciation) in a firm's other financial statements, which are essentially book-entry items for which there is no commensurate flow of cash, hence the need for a cash flow statement which shows the actual sources and uses of cash during a given accounting period. We present below the cash flow statement for the same company we have already considered.

		current year		previous year	
Consolidated cash flow statement Year ended 31st May current year					
	Note	£'000	£'000	£'000	£'000
Cash inflow from operating activities	21		**8,600**		_4,211_
Returns on investments and servicing of finance					
Interest received		**14**		_29_	
Interest paid		**(521)**		_(221)_	
Interest element of hire purchase and finance lease payments		**(11)**		_(25)_	
Dividend paid		**(75)**		_(321)_	
Net cash outflow from returns on investments and servicing of finance			**(593)**		_(538)_
Tax paid					
Advance corporation tax		**(19)**		_(93)_	
Corporation tax		**(215)**		_(55)_	
			(234)		_(148)_
Investing activities					
Payments to acquire players' registrations		**(8,409)**		_(4,676)_	
Receipts from sales of players' registrations		**4,035**		_3,430_	
			(4,374)		_(1,246)_
Payments to acquire tangible fixed assets		**(8,432)**		_(3,396)_	
Receipts from sales of tangible fixed assets		**76**		_64_	
Receipts from sales of properties for resale		**225**		_—_	
			(8,131)		_(3,332)_
Net cash outflow from investing activities			**(12,505)**		_(4,578)_
Net cash outflow before financing			**(4,732)**		_(1,053)_
Financing					
Net increase in obligations under hire purchase and lease obligations	23	**1,606**		_38_	
Bank loan drawn down	23	**2,400**		_2,600_	
Bank loan repayments	23	**(750)**		_—_	
other loans drawn down	23	**1,800**		_—_	
Other loans repaid	23	**(1,550)**		_—_	
			3,506		_2,638_
(Decrease)/increase in cash and cash equivalents			**(1,226)**		_1,585_

The notes on pages xx to zz form part of these financial statements.

2.5   Taxation and Inflation

A substantial amount of any firm's resources is devoted to dealing with taxation. Indeed, some would argue that not only do firms have to pay taxes, but that they are also required to devote too much of their time and energies to dealing with the bureaucracy imposed by the tax authorities. Tax significantly affects a firm's decisions, especially its financial decisions. This is made all the more onerous because the tax system tends to change annually. In the United Kingdom, the Chancellor of the Exchequer announces changes to the tax system in his annual Budget speech to Parliament. This normally occurs during March.

In principle, governments would prefer changes in taxation to be neutral; that is to say, that taxation itself would not be a major determinant in economic decision-making. In reality however, taxation tends not to be neutral, serving instead to "distort" economic activity as individuals and firms make decisions based primarily on minimising their tax liability.

In order to make sound financial decisions, it is important for stakeholders in a firm to remain well-informed about taxation. This is especially the case for the finance manager and those who invest their monies in a firm. For small firms, the accountant is often the primary source of taxation information. So, what taxes must the firm take account of in its decision-making?

Taxes can be either direct or indirect; the former are usually levied on incomes, whilst the latter usually take the form of a sales tax or value-added tax. In most modern economies, income taxes (including corporate income tax) are usually progressive—whereby those better able to pay (considered as those with higher incomes) pay tax at a higher rate—while indirect taxes are regressive—people are taxed at the same rate regardless of their ability to pay. In what follows only the most basic of features are covered; full details are much more complex, an indication as to why the services of accountants are so highly regarded and in high demand in many countries.

2.5.1   Personal taxation

In most economies, individual incomes above a minimum level are subject to personal income tax. In the United Kingdom, this threshold for an individual taxpayer (known as the personal allowance) was as follows:

1992–1993	1995–1996	1996–1997	1999–2000	2000–2001	2001–2002
£3,445	£3,525	£3,765	£4,335	£4,385	£4,535

A different level of allowance exists for married couples, those between the ages of 65 and 74, and for those over the age of 75. Full details can be found on the Inland Revenue website at www.inlandrevenue.gov.uk/rates/it.htm.

Taxable income may differ from an individual's actual income because certain expenditures may be allowable against tax. For example, payments into an occupational pension scheme are deducted from income before income tax is levied. Other deductions in the United Kingdom include some kinds of charitable donations out of payroll. In the past, some tax-deductibility of mortgage interest payments to encourage home ownership existed known as MIRAS (Mortgage Interest Relief At Source). In the United States, such items as medical payments, some educational expenses and charitable donations are tax-deductible.

Some economies also like to distinguish between earned and unearned (or investment) income for taxation purposes. However, currently in the United Kingdom these sources of income are taxed equivalently. There are three bands of personal income tax rate, payable on income above the taxpayer's allowance:

10% on the lowest levels of income ("the starting rate")
22% "the basic rate", payable on the 'middle' range of incomes
40% "the higher rate", payable on 'higher' incomes.

In the past, the top rate of personal income tax in the UK has been as high as 90%!! In theory, both tax rates and allowances are adjusted to account for the rate of inflation. The reality is somewhat more *ad hoc*:

	2001–2002	2002–2003	2003–2004
Starting rate, 10%	£0 – £1,880	£0 – £1,920	£0 – £1,960
Basic rate, 22%	£1,881 – £29,400	£1,921 – £29,900	£1,961 – £30,500
Higher rate, 40%	Over £29,400	Over £29,900	Over £30,500

In addition to the personal income tax sthere is also a payroll tax in many countries. This is known as National Insurance Contributions (NIC) in the United Kingdom, and is paid by both the employer and employee. These contributions are meant to provide funding for the state pension, the National Health Service (NHS) and other welfare benefits. In truth, these monies have never been ring-fenced, and have rarely provided enough money for the services they are meant to fund. Full details on NICs can be found at www.inlandrevenue.gov.uk/rates/ nic.htm.

2.5.2 Capital gains tax

While investment income due to interest or dividend payments is subject to personal income tax, financial investments (for example, shares and bonds) may also provide their holder with a capital gain when they are sold. Capital gains which are realised through the sale of real assets or securities and are above a given threshold (known as the annual exemption) are subject to capital gains tax at a rate equal to the highest rate of personal income tax. Trading losses in one year can be set against gains made in the current and following year. Annual exemption for individuals is as follows:

1992–1994	2001–2002	2002–2003	2003–2004
£5,800	£7,500	£7,700	£7,900

2.5.3 Corporation tax

Corporations are liable for taxation on their earnings in much the same way as individuals on their incomes. Companies also pay corporation tax on a graduated basis. Like individuals, corporations may find some of their expenditures tax-deductible. Thus, for most purposes and in many economies, corporation tax and income tax work in much the same manner. For several years, the main rate of corporation tax in the United Kingdom has been 30%. A lower rate of 19% exists for smaller companies, defined (2002–2004) as companies with taxable profits between £50,000 and £300,000. Similarly, there is now a zero rate for companies with taxable profits below £10,000. This was previously set at

10%. Earlier levels of corporate tax rates are summarised in the following table:

Table 2: Corporate Tax Rates

1966–1968	42.5%
1968–1970	45.0%
1970–1971	42.5%
1971–1973	40.0%
1973–1983	52.0% (includes imputed tax)
1983–1984	50.0% (includes imputed tax)
1984–1985	52.0% (includes imputed tax)
1985–1986	45.0% (includes imputed tax)
1986–1990	40.0% (includes imputed tax)
1990–1992	35.0% (includes imputed tax)
1992–1997	33.0% (includes imputed tax)
1997–1999	31.0% (includes imputed tax)
Since 1999	30.0%

The phrase "imputed tax" refers to the system of Advanced Corporation Tax (ACT) which was abolished from 6th April, 1999.

2.5.5   Inflation
There is a great deal of misconception about the meaning of inflation. When a person's favourite product has gone up in price there is a tendency to blame the increase on inflation. While this may indeed be the case, it might also be simply a case of increased demand for that particular product. In order to make sound economic and financial decisions, we must be able to distinguish clearly between a price increase and inflation.

Inflation is normally defined as a "sustained increase in the general level of prices". The general level of prices refers to a weighted average of the prices of all goods. It is entirely feasible for this average to be rising, and the price of your favourite good to be falling at the same time, or even *vice versa*. In the United Kingdom, the general level of prices is proxied by the Retail Price Index (RPI). However, note that for inflation to be occurring the increase in the general level must be "sustained".

That means the prices must be rising in general over a lengthy period of time, such as a year or more.

Before the Second World War (1939–1945), the business cycle was such that inflation and growth tended to move together. Thus, when the economy was in recession, the general level of prices would also be in decline; that is, there would be **deflation**. The post-War era has been characterised by almost continuous inflation, especially for most Western countries. As economic growth takes place inflation occurs; as growth increases in pace, inflation increases as well. When there has been recession, there has been disinflation: a reduction in the rate of inflation.

An increase in the general level of prices is tantamount to a reduction in the value of a unit of currency. Thus, when there is inflation, a pound will buy you less today than it did a year ago. There has been a reduction in its purchasing power. Consequently, if a firm is making greater profits this year than the previous year, it becomes crucial to understand whether this is due to better performance by the company or simply the result of inflation. In the early part of the 1970s, it was often the case that a company with higher profits due to inflation would find itself in a higher tax bracket. Nowadays, tax thresholds tend to move in line with the rate of inflation to offset such effects. Nonetheless, this illustrates the impact that inflation can have on a company's finances. One way of dealing with the impact of inflation is to distinguish between real and nominal values:

Real values and nominal values
Nominal value refers to the value of a commodity (its price) measured in terms of the currency unit (pounds sterling) today. Nominal values can be said to be misleading, as they do not take into account inflation. Most company accounts are prepared on the (implicit) assumption that prices are stable. To remedy this nominal values can be converted into real values to take into account the rate of inflation.

Real values are prices measured in terms of the value of the currency at a given point in time. So real values might be calculated based on what the pound would buy in a given "base year", say 2000. While there have been attempts to prepare company accounts using real values, no degree of agreement has been reached as to the best way of achieving a consistent method of adjusting for the distortions occasioned by inflation.

Most financial calculations today are performed in terms of nominal values. While some of this is due to the more stable inflationary environment since the 1990s, it is also due to the fact that conversion to real values brings along its own set of methodological issues, often raising more questions than we were seeking to answer in the first place. For example, one can convert nominal values into real values by use of any one of a number of proxies for the general price level: the Retail Price Index (RPI) and the Gross Domestic Product deflator being prime examples. Which index is used is a matter of choice, but therefore also subject to criticism.

What is beyond question is the need for consistency. In making financial calculations by which decisions are guided it is crucial either to use real values throughout, or to use nominal values throughout. Like oil and water, real and nominal values do not mix well together.

Appendix: Sources of Financial Information

Traditional "print" media

While most of the broadsheet newspapers in the United Kingdom offer good coverage of key business and financial news and a selection of overnight closing prices on a range of securities, the *Financial Times* (*FT*) remains the authoritative daily source of information about the financial system both at home and abroad. Immediately recognisable by its individualistic pink pages, the *FT* also offers equally authoritative coverage of broader news items. Despite their UK origins, both the *FT* and *The Economist* offer excellent coverage of the world as it goes about its business.

Although regarded by some as a magazine, *The Economist* is a weekly news journal, and remains one of the best sources of both information and analysis of key business and financial events. Because of its weekly format, it can provide a greater level of depth in consideration of contemporary issues. *The Economist* is also well-noted for its regular series of Surveys and Schools Briefs; the former covering such topics as Investment Banking, Central Banking, or perhaps even analysis of a particular country; the latter offers an up-to-date insight into a particular area of economic science, such as monetary union or the minimum wage. Each week, *The Economist* has an entire section devoted to business and another to finance and economics.

Both the *Financial Times* and *The Economist* are available online (i.e. via the Internet). Although not all of their services are free, both offer enough up-to-date news and data even for the non-paying web-surfer. The URLs for these and some other sites of interest appear at the end of this Appendix.

Published daily except Sundays, the *Financial Times* offers a weekday format and a (different) weekend format. The weekday edition is strong on news items, while the weekend edition takes a more in-depth look at the previous week's issues. Indeed, the weekend edition also includes greater coverage of sports, fashion and the arts, in addition to analysis of the week's financial and economic affairs. In both weekday and weekend editions, a series of *FT* columnists offer analysis, opinion, and occasional glances at research findings in academia or government. The Monday edition also takes a slightly different format, when a more considered analysis of the previous week's market trends is undertaken.

Online and broadcast media

It is often acknowledged that we live in an "age of information", and this information is increasingly disseminated by electronic means. Earlier this century radio broadcasts began, followed by television in the second half of the century. The final decade of the twentieth century witnessed an explosion of computer-based online services, from proprietary services such as CompuServe and America Online (AOL) to the Internet. Digital provision of information to a PC via a modem or broadband offers the user immediate access both to the information available in traditional media and much, much more besides. Satellite and cable television also offer a range of news sources, from the generalised 24 hour news services to specialised financial channels such as CNBC and Bloomberg.

America Online, the Motley Fool and more

America Online (AOL) is the world's largest online service, with most of its subscribers located in the United States. The most popular site within AOL is "Motley Fool", an investment forum set up and run by Tom and David Gardner, two brothers with a keen interest in the financial marketplace. Named after the court jester in Shakespeare's *As You Like It*, this forum offers a wide range of financial information, from basic information for new investors, to online share prices, immediate news headlines, downloadable software, and everything the investor could need to become more informed. Each night the brothers analyse the day's (New York) market activity, and show how their own portfolio is doing (they have put their money where their digital mouth is!). The Motley Fool also provides investment education in an online format, and is increasingly established in localised format with local content for particular countries.

The most intriguing aspect of the Motley Fool site is its various message boards and the "chat room". The message boards offer a forum by which AOL subscribers can request or post information, as well as news, views, and trivia for other AOL subscribers to read. It has been known for directors and managing directors of major listed companies to come into the chat room and respond to questions from interested parties.

The Motley Fool is also available via a website at www.fool.com, but this does not offer the full range available to AOL subscribers.

In addition to AOL, there are a wide range of web sites offering all manner of information as well as online financial services, from banking to stockbroking and foreign exchange trading. One result of this vast array of information has been the development of an industry of "day traders", amateur investors who try to make profits by playing the various financial markets typically by using one or more of the online brokerages. Financial information providers, such as Reuters and Bloomberg, also offer online services including daily or weekly e-mail newsletters in addition to their satellite digital television programming.

Table 3: Some key URLs of interest in Finance

The Economist	www.economist.com
The Financial Times	www.ft.com
The Electronic Telegraph	www.telegraph.co.uk
The Wall Street Journal	www.wsj.com
Reuters (UK)	www.reuters.co.uk
Bloomberg	www.bloomberg.co.uk
Yahoo! Finance (UK & Ireland)	uk.finance.yahoo.com
H.M. Treasury Directory Index	www.hm-treasury.gov.uk
The Inland Revenue (UK)	www.inlandrevenue.gov.uk
The London Stock Exchange	www.londonstockexchange.com
Alternative Investment Market	www.londonstockexchange.com/aim
The Institute of Chartered Accountants	www.icaew.org.uk
Euronext•LIFFE	www.liffe.com
The World Bank Home Page	www.worldbank.org
The International Monetary Fund (IMF)	www.imf.org

As well as the sites listed above there is a plethora of other sites of interest, offering everything from glossaries in finance to practical investment advice, and even online calculators for pricing derivatives. Many finance instructors make their own work available via the web. The best way to find any site is to make use of one of the many search engines available, such as Google, Yahoo, Lycos, and so on. However, bear in mind that unless a website is published by a reputable source, there is no guarantee of the quality of the information it provides.

3.   Value: Finance Foundations

It has been said the entire edifice of finance is built upon the concept of value. Indeed, a large part of the finance literature is concerned with defining and refining techniques for calculating value: i.e. valuation techniques. As we have already discussed, the main objective of the firm is to maximise its value, so valuation techniques are an important part of the financial specialist's toolkit. The most important economic decisions are those which involve investment in real assets, whether by individuals or by companies, as the impact is truly long-lasting. The key to making such decisions lies in deciding whether the particular asset will add value. And we have already noted that the true objective of the firm is to maximise its value, thereby maximising shareholder wealth.

3.1   What Is Value?

The concept of value is one which has bedevilled philosophers since the dawn of time. There is a natural human instinct to value things subjectively; this is why what one individual regards as a bargain, another would consider exploitation. Following more than two hundred years of inquiry and debate, economists argue that value is reflected in the price of a commodity, as determined by the interaction of supply and demand. This measure of value is objective, and reconciles the conflicting subjective values of all "players" in the market.

However, the value of a commodity is not static. Values vary over time as supply and demand conditions change. If this were not the case, the value of a commodity today would be the same as the value of that same commodity in the future. But there is more to it than this for the unique commodity known as money.

Given the choice of receiving (say) £100 today or a year from now, most people would ask for the money now! It follows that any given sum of money is considered to be worth more if received today than if it were to be received in the future. Part of this is due to **uncertainty**; at its most extreme the receiver will not be sure that he will live to collect the sum! It is one reason why people tend to prefer "jam today" over "jam tomorrow".

This remains true even in the presence of positive inflation, when money's purchasing power is not maintained. This difference in the value of money at different points in time is reflected in the rate of interest; the rate of interest may be seen as the market's determination of **the time value of money**. Thus, a given sum of money today—the **principal**—is equivalent in value to that sum of money plus what it could earn in interest payments. Thus, if we are to truly understand value we must begin with an understanding of interest. Interest can be earned on loans in two ways: simple interest, and compound interest. We consider these in turn.

3.2   The Time Value of Money I: Simple Interest

When only the principal earns interest over the life of a transaction, the interest earned is referred to as **simple interest**. So if:

   P = the principal

   r = the rate of interest (*per annum*, unless otherwise stated)

and T = the time period for which the principal is invested, then the interest due, I, is given by

$$I = P * r * T$$

Example:

Consider a sum of £1,000 invested at 8% for 60 days. The interest due will be

$$I = P * r * T$$

$$I = £1,000 * \frac{8}{100} * \frac{60}{365} = £13.15$$

At the end of the period the investor would have both principal (£1,000) and interest (£13.15), giving a total of £1,013.15.

Note that because the interest is stated on an annual (*per annum*) basis, we measure the time of the investment in annual terms. If the interest were quoted semi-annually we would measure the time of the investment in six-monthly periods. This **dimensional consistency** is crucial. In more general terms, it follows that:

$$FV = P + I$$

future value = principal + interest

Thus, because $FV = P + I$

and $I = P \times r \times T$, then:

$$FV = P(1 + rT)$$

Example:

What is the future value of £700 invested at 10% for 2 years?

$$FV = P(1 + rT)$$
$$FV = 700(1 + [0.1*2])$$
$$FV = £840$$

It is also possible to calculate **the rate of return** or **yield** on a simple interest loan. Let:

FV = the final sum received
P = the principal invested
T = the time period for which the principal is invested.

Then the rate of return (in %) earned over time T is given by:

$$\frac{FV - P}{P} * 100$$

Because some simple interest loans may be for periods of less than one year, it is convenient to be able to calculate the rate of return on an **annualised** basis:

$$\frac{FV - P}{P} * 100 * \frac{365}{T}$$

Example:

Consider a simple interest loan of £1,000 for 60 days. The principal, P, is £1,000, and T = 60 days.

If the loan has a future value, FV, of £1,013.15, then, the rate of return is

$$\frac{1,013.15 - 1,000}{1,000} * 100 = 1.315\%$$

and the annualised rate of return is $1.315 \times \dfrac{365}{60} = 8\%$, as expected.

3.3   Simple Interest: Applications

3.3.1   Term loans

As with individuals, for many companies the first source of (short-term) funding is the overdraft facility extended by the bank. Indeed, for small and medium-size enterprises (SMEs) it may be the only source. But there is a major drawback for firms relying on overdraft facilities, as they may be removed "on demand". One alternative—which emerged in the USA during the 1970s, particularly for larger companies—is to seek funding via term loans. Term loans are for an agreed sum (the **principal**) lent for a fixed term, and may involve both interest payments and a fee.

Term loans usually incur interest on a floating rate basis plus a margin. In Britain there are two major floating base rates:

London InterBank Offer Rate (LIBOR) is the market rate which banks pay in order to obtain marginal funds in the inter-bank money market. LIBOR fluctuates swiftly in response to changing supply and demand conditions. LIBOR is predominantly used in large transactions.

Base Rate refers to a composite rate charged by the commercial banks, consisting of the return offered to depositors plus a spread to cover administrative costs, etc. Base Rate changes infrequently, and is the anchor rate for smaller transactions, including overdrafts and personal loans.

In both cases the margin charged is supposed to reflect such items as the borrower's creditworthiness and the size of the transaction, both reflections of the risk involved. This is not always the case in practice.

Interest on term loans is typically calculated using simple interest. For LIBOR-related transactions the repayments may be based on quarterly or six-monthly intervals. The interest payable on such a loan would be:

$$\text{Principal} * [\text{LIBOR} + \text{margin}] * \left\{ \frac{\text{loan period (days)}}{365} \right\}$$

3.3.2 Discount claims

Financial claims traded in the money market are typically traded at a **discount**. They may offer no interest, in which case the discount provides the only source of gain for the purchaser. It is the difference between the maturity value and the purchase price that forms the discount. Examples of instruments traded on a discount basis include Bills of Exchange, Treasury Bills, UK local authority bills, Bankers' Acceptances, and commercial paper (particularly in the United States). They are usually quoted on a *per annum* discount rate basis.

Example:

Suppose there is a discount of 8% on a £100,000 bill for 91 days. Then the discount is as follows:

$$\text{Discount} = £100,000 * \frac{08}{100} * \frac{91}{365} = £1,994.52$$

Thus the purchaser would pay £(100,000 − 1,994.52) = £98,005.48 and receive £100,000 on maturity. The rate of return earned (i.e., the true yield) would be:

$$\frac{\text{maturity value} - \text{purchase price}}{\text{purchase price}} * \frac{365}{t} * 100 =$$

$$\frac{100,000 - 98,005.48}{98,005.48} * \frac{365}{91} * 100 = 8.16\%$$

Note that the true yield will always be higher than the discount rate.

For companies which are large (assets over £25 million) and well-known (a stock exchange listing), an alternative source of funds is via the issue of **commercial paper (CP)**. Commercial paper is directly-issued short-term debt in the form of unsecured promissory notes, with a maturity between seven days and one year. CP is usually sold on a discount basis. These criteria are much the same as for the issuance of medium-term notes, which have a maturity between one year and five years.

Because companies who issue CP or medium-term notes are going directly via the financial markets to lenders, thereby avoiding borrowing from financial intermediaries such as banks, the process is sometimes referred to as one of "disintermediation".

Typically, a company will have an agreement with a syndicate of banks that permit it to issue CP at short notice and for varying amounts (a minimum of £100,000 is required) and varying maturities (91 days or less is common in the UK; somewhat longer is the norm in the USA). The banks in turn will either keep the CP or, more likely, sell it on to investors. The funding cost to the company is lower than that of an overdraft, but the process is less flexible. The return to the investor is higher than that on government-issued bills, for example, but there is an associated corporate credit risk involved.

3.3.3   Yield-quoted instruments

Perhaps the most well-known instrument quoted on a yield basis is the **Certificate of Deposit** (CD). CDs became particularly popular in the USA during the deregulatory period of the 1980s, and are often seen as another form of **time deposit** with a bank. A CD is essentially a receipt for a deposit made with an issuing bank, which states the principal, nominal rate of interest, date of issue, and maturity date. CDs are typically bearer instruments, and negotiable without endorsement.

The return offered on a CD is normally higher than on a similar government-issued bond, even though the risks are not perceived as much greater due to the existence of the underlying deposit. There exists a fairly efficient secondary market for prime bank CDs, which is often used by companies as a haven for short-term surplus funds by way of an alternative to using "traditional" bank deposits. Made by bankers and brokers in London, the active secondary market helps maintain liquidity, increasing the attraction of these claims.

The value of a (sterling) CD on maturity is:

$$\text{Value} = \text{principal} * \left[1 + \left\{ r * \left(\frac{\text{life in days}}{365} \right) \right\} \right]$$

where *r* is the nominal interest rate in per cent.

The value of the CD on the secondary market, however, would be:

$$\text{Value} = \text{principal} * \left[\frac{\left[1 + \left\{ r * \left(\dfrac{\text{life in days}}{365} \right) \right\} \right]}{1 + \left\{ \text{yield} * \left(\dfrac{\text{remaining days}}{365} \right) \right\}} \right]$$

It is worth noting that the "day count" differs in various countries. For example, while a year is counted as 365 days under United Kingdom financial market conventions, United States' dollar CDs are based on a 360-day year.

Example:

Consider a 90-day CD with a nominal principal of $50,000, issued at a nominal rate of interest of 8%. If the CD was bought at issue, held for 60 days, and then sold on a yield of 9%, the proceeds would be:

$$\text{Price} = \$50,000 * \left[\frac{\left[1 + \left\{ 8\% * \left(\dfrac{90}{360} \right) \right\} \right]}{1 + \left\{ 9\% * \left(\dfrac{30}{360} \right) \right\}} \right] = \$50,620.35$$

and the annualised rate of return would be:

$$\frac{620.35 * 360 * 100}{50,000 * 60} = 7.44\%$$

3.4   The Time Value of Money II: Compound Interest

3.4.1   The mechanics of compound interest

Unlike simple interest, compound interest works on the premise that interest payments are reinvested and earn the same rate of interest as the principal. Thus, compound interest implies that both principal and interest earn interest. Historians have traced the use of compound interest far back into antiquity, even as long ago as c.1800 BC where, for example, it was used by traders in Babylon. The best way to understand compound interest is through an example.

Example:

Let P = the principal = £1,000

r = the rate of interest (*per annum*) = 10%

T = the number of time periods for which the principal is invested

= 3 years

Then the interest, I, due at the end of year 1, is given by

$$I = P_1 * r * T$$

which gives at the end of year 1 a total of

$$P_1 + 1 = £1,000 + £100 = £1,100$$

The investor now has P_2 = £1,100 as principal available for investment in year 2. Thus, at the end of year 2 the interest earned will be

$$I = P_2 * r * T$$

giving at the end of year 2 a total of

$$P_2 + I = £1,100 + £110 = £1,210$$

Thus, by the end of year 3 the wealth will have accumulated to

$$P_3 + I = £1,210 + £121 = £1,331$$

i.e. interest earned over the entire 3-year period is £331, which is £31 more than would have been earned via simple interest.

In general terms the following will prevail:

end year 1: $P(1 + r)$

end year 2: $P(1 + r)(1 + r) = P(1 + r)^2$

end year 3: $P(1 + r)(1 + r)(1 + r) = P(1 + r)^3$

Extrapolating this pattern we find

$$FV_T = P(1 + r)^T$$

Naturally, if interest is paid several times a year (say n times) then for dimensional consistency this formula needs to be adjusted accordingly to give

$$FV_T = P\left(1 + \frac{r}{n}\right)^{n*T}$$

Example:

Consider £1,000 invested for $8\frac{1}{2}$ years at 17% *per annum*, compounded quarterly. Applying the formula immediately above, we obtain:

$$FV_T = £1,000\left(1 + \frac{0.17}{4}\right)^{4*8.5}$$

$$FV_T = £1,000(4.11705) = £4,117.05$$

Recall, the true or effective yield *per annum* is:

$$\frac{FV - P}{P} * 100$$

$$= \frac{P\left(1 + \frac{r}{n}\right)^n - P}{P} * 100 = \left(1 + \frac{r}{n}\right)^n - 1$$

or, over T years the total yield $= \left(1 + \frac{r}{n}\right)^{nT} - 1.$

Practitioners in the markets find that certain special cases of these formulae are more common than others. For example, it is often extremely useful to be able to switch easily between annual yields and semi-annual yields. Thus, if r_A = annual compound yield, and r_S = semi-annual compound yield, then

$$\left(1 + \frac{r_A}{100}\right) = \left(1 + \frac{r_S}{100}\right)^2$$

A simple example might be as follows:

Semi-annual %	8.00	10.00	12.00	14.00	16.00
Annual %	8.16	10.25	12.36	14.49	16.64

3.4.2   Comparing simple and compound interest

Although it appears quite simple mechanically, there is a power to compounding that belies imagination. In 1959 S. Branch Walker of Stamford, Connecticut wrote a letter to *Life* magazine in the United States, which illustrated this power by applying compound interest to a well-known tale from north American history:

> Sirs:
> The Indian who sold Manhattan for $24.00 was a sharp salesman. If he had put his $24 away at 6% compounded semiannually, it would now be $9.5 billion and could buy most of the now-improved land back.   [*Life*, August 31, 1959]

By now you should be able to calculate for yourself how much $9.5 billion in 1959 would be worth today if compounded semi-annually at 6%. We can illustrate the power of compounding using a much simpler example.

Example:

Consider a principal, *P*, of £1,000. Suppose the rate of interest is 8% *per annum*. What will be the future value annually for the next ten years under both simple interest and compound interest?

Begin by constructing a table of values:

Year	1	2	3	4	5	6	7	8	9	10
Simple interest	1,080	1,160	1,240	1,320	1,400	1,480	1,560	1,640	1,720	1,800
Compound interest	1,080	1,166	1,260	1,360	1,469	1,587	1,714	1,851	1,999	2,159

and then plot these values on a graph. This really shows the power of compound interest:

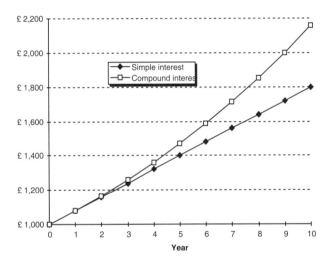

There are a couple of simple deductions worth making based on observing this graph. Firstly, for relatively short periods of time there is little difference between the future value based on simple interest and that on compound interest. This might well account for the fact that short-term debt tends to be based on simple interest, whereas longer-term debt is almost exclusively based on compound interest. Secondly, the longer the passage of time the more lucrative is compound interest vis-à-vis simple interest. With a higher rate of interest this difference would become even more pronounced.

3.4.3 Annuities

In the foregoing we considered the future value of a single sum of money which earned interest. We now consider the case of an annuity.

An annuity is typically defined as an asset paying a fixed amount of money each year (the term is obviously derived from the payments being annual). However, we can also define an annuity more broadly as any finite series of cash flows of a constant sum. This applies equally, whether or not the payments are being received (as is the case with the traditional definition) or if they are being made. We can calculate the future value of an annuity using the following formula:

$$FV = CF\left[\frac{(1 + r)^T - 1}{r}\right]$$

where CF = the amount of the periodic payment (cashflow), r = the rate of interest, and T = the life-span of the annuity. It is worth recalling that T and r must be dimensionally consistent, so that if T is measured in years then r represents the annual rate of interest; if if T is measured in months then r represents the monthly rate of interest; and so on.

Example:

You are currently saving €100 each month, and wish to know how much you will have saved in five years' time. The prevailing rate of interest on your savings account is 5 per cent *per annum*. Applying the formula above, we find:

$$FV = €100\left[\frac{\left(1 + \dfrac{0.05}{12}\right)^{5*12} - 1}{\dfrac{0.05}{12}}\right]$$

$$FV = €100\left[\frac{(1 + 0.004166667)^{60} - 1}{0.004166667}\right] = €6,800.61$$

All of this applies to a regular or ordinary annuity, for which the cash flows are paid (or received) at the *end* of each time period. We can also define an **annuity due** as an annuity for which the cash flows are paid (or received) at the *beginning* of each time period. The future value of an annuity due is simply the future value of an ordinary annuity compounded for an additional time period. Thus for an annuity due over *T* periods we find:

$$FV_T^{due} = FV_T^{ordinary}(1 + r)$$

3.5 Net Present Value and Internal Rate of Return

3.5.1 Net Present Value

Compounding allows us to see what a given sum of money today will be worth at some time in the future. It is a process of looking forward along a timeline. **Discounting** is a reversal of that process, looking backwards along a timeline. Discounting allows us to calculate present value: what a given sum of money to be received in the future is worth today. Diagrammatically this can be visualised as follows:

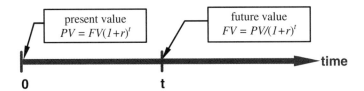

From compounding we know that

$$FV = P(1 + r)^T$$

If we invert the compounding formula, we obtain:

$$PV = \frac{FV}{(1 + r)^T}$$

This tells us that an amount of money equal to *FV* being received *T* periods from now is equivalent to the sum of *PV* today, if the rate of interest is *r*. The rate of interest is a measure of the cost of acquiring funds—that is the "cost of capital"—and is known in this context as the "discount rate". It should be quite apparent from the formula that there will be an inverse relationship between the discount rate and the relevant present value: higher discount rates will lead to lower present values, and *vice versa*.

The formula suggests that a rational investor would be indifferent between receiving *PV* today or *FV* in the future. This is also referred to as *PV* being the present value of *FV* received *T* years from now, where $1/(1 + r)^T$ is known as the **discount factor** or **present value interest factor**, PVIF. Older textbooks, and newer editions of older texts, often print tables of discount factors as Appendices. This is largely a hangover from the days before hand-held calculators were cheap and plentiful, and offered a more convenient means of calculating present values in much the same way that older mathematics texts printed tables of logarithms. A sample of such a PVIF table is presented below:

Period	1%	2%	3%	4%	5%	6%	7%	8%
1	0.9901	0.9804	0.9709	0.9615	0.9524	0.9434	0.9346	0.9259
2	0.9803	0.9612	0.9426	0.9246	0.9070	0.8900	0.8734	0.8573
3	0.9706	0.9423	0.9151	0.8890	0.8638	0.8396	0.8163	0.7938
4	0.9610	0.9238	0.8885	0.8548	0.8227	0.7921	0.7629	0.7350
5	0.9515	0.9057	0.8626	0.8219	0.7835	0.7473	0.7130	0.6806
6	0.9420	0.8880	0.8375	0.7903	0.7462	0.7050	0.6663	0.6302
7	0.9327	0.8706	0.8131	0.7599	0.7107	0.6651	0.6227	0.5835
8	0.9235	0.8535	0.7894	0.7307	0.6768	0.6274	0.5820	0.5403
9	0.9143	0.8368	0.7664	0.7026	0.6446	0.5919	0.5439	0.5002
10	0.9053	0.8203	0.7441	0.6756	0.6139	0.5584	0.5083	0.4632
11	0.8963	0.8043	0.7224	0.6496	0.5847	0.5268	0.4751	0.4289
12	0.8874	0.7885	0.7014	0.6246	0.5568	0.4970	0.4440	0.3971

As with most applications of mathematical techniques, the numerical nature of financial calculations means that the best way to get to grips with present value is by example.

Example 1:

Find the present value (*PV*) of £2,000 due in 6 years if interest rates are 10% *per annum*, compounded semi-annually.

$$PV = \frac{£2,000}{(1.05)^{12}} = \frac{£2,000}{1.79586} = £1,113.67$$

This example shows the calculation of present value for a single future cashflow. The same is true of the next example, although it is of a slightly more complex form:

Example 2:

> If current interest rates are 10% *per annum*, what is the *PV* of a debt of
> £2,500 due in 8 years, with interest being compounded at 6% quarterly?
>
> i) Begin by calculating what the debt will be worth when it is due, that is to
> say the *FV* of the debt:
>
> $$FV = £2,500(1.015)^{32} = £4,025.81$$
>
> ii) Now calculate the PV of the debt from (i)
>
> $$= \frac{£4,025.81}{(1.10)^8} = \frac{£4,025.81}{2.14359} = £1,787.07$$

The next stage of complexity involves calculating the present value of a **stream of cashflows** that occur during a number of years (or periods) in the future. Note that present value offers us a common denominator under which we can bring together future sums of money. Thus, we calculate individually the present value of each of the individual future cashflows, and then sum them. If C_t represents the cashflow during year t from an investment that lasts for T years, then the present value of that investment would be:

$$PV = -C_0 + PV(C_1) + PV(C_2) + PV(C_3) + \ldots + PV(C_T)$$

$$PV = -C_0 + \frac{C_1}{(1 + r)} + \frac{C_2}{(1 + r)^2} + \frac{C_3}{(1 + r)^3} + \ldots + \frac{C_T}{(1 + r)^T}$$

$$PV = -C_0 + \sum_{t=1}^{T} \frac{C_t}{(1 + r)^t}$$

Note that the initial cashflow is negative; "traditional" investments are those where negative cashflow (payment) in the first period leads to positive net cashflows in successive periods. Thus, instead of being referred to as "Present Value" (PV), the term "Net Present Value" (NPV) is often used. Ignoring the sign of the first-period cashflow:

$$NPV = \sum_{t=0}^{T} \frac{C_t}{(1 + r)^t}$$

The "rule" used in making decisions is that investments which offer a positive Net Present Value are worth undertaking: they will add value to the firm or the individual's net wealth by the exact amount of the NPV.

Example:

You have the opportunity to invest £9,000 which over the next five years will return £1,000, £2,000, £3,000, £5,000, and £4,000 respectively. If the discount rate (i.e., the prevailing rate of interest) is 12%, is this a worthwhile investment?

First, set up the NPV equation:

$$NPV = -£9,000 + \frac{£1,000}{(1 + 0.12)} + \frac{£2,000}{(1 + 0.12)^2} + \frac{£3,000}{(1 + 0.12)^3}$$

$$+ \frac{£5,000}{(1 + 0.12)^4} + \frac{£4,000}{(1 + 0.12)^5}$$

NPV = −£9,000 + £892.86 + £1,594.39 + £2,135.34 + £3,177.59 + £2,269.71

NPV = −£9,000 + £10,069.88 = £1,069.88

Because the NPV is positive, this investment has positive (net present) value, and is therefore worthwhile.

3.5.2   "Special" cashflow streams

The technique of calculating present value allows us to see what a stream of future cashflows is worth today. However, different investments offer very different cashflow profiles, both in terms of amount and of timing. While many investments offer cashflows with uneven payments in terms of amount, some financial investments have a time-profile which offers a more even stream of payments.

Perpetuities

Most loans have a finite lifespan, at the end of which the principal is repaid. However, some loans take the form of perpetual loans, or "perpetuities", whereby there is no repayment of principal. This is because a perpetuity is an annuity with an infinite lifespan, i.e., a series of (equal) cashflows which never terminate (see Section 3.4.3). People are often amazed to find that there actually are perpetual loans in existence, because the implication is that the lender is never repaid the amount being lent. The most well-known of all perpetuities in existence are British government undated bonds, commonly known as "Consols". Originally there was a very large issue of these perpetual gilts by the British government following the Napoleonic Wars (1815). The aim was to make use of the proceeds to redeem the bonds from other, smaller issues which had been used to finance the war, thereby consolidating the government's debt. Hence, "Consols".

Consider then a series of infinite cashflows, with a view to finding the present value. The formula is adapted thus:

$$PV = PV(C_1) + PV(C_2) + PV(C_3) + \ldots + PV(C_\infty)$$

However, because a Consol is a form of annuity, the coupon payments are the same in each time period: $C_1 = C_2 = C_3 = \ldots = C_\infty = C$. Thus:

$$PV = \frac{C}{(1+r)} + \frac{C}{(1+r)^2} + \frac{C}{(1+r)^3} + \cdots + \frac{C}{(1+r)^\infty}$$

$$PV = \sum_{t=1}^{\infty} \frac{C}{(1+r)^t} = C\left[\sum_{t=1}^{\infty} \frac{1}{(1+r)^t}\right]$$

which simplifies to $PV = \dfrac{C}{r}$.

Example:

You have been offered the chance to purchase a British government Consol which pays an annual coupon of £1,000. If the prevailing rate of interest (the appropriate discount rate) is 7%, what is the most you would be willing to pay for this Consol?

$$PV = \frac{C}{r} = \frac{£1,000}{0.07} = £14,285.72$$

The most you should be willing to pay for this Consol is its present value: £14,285.72.

If market conditions were such that the market price of a Consol were lower than its present value, then the Consol would be considered "underpriced" and hence a bargain. Presumably, such a discrepancy would be noticed by a large number of people, who would try to buy the Consol, increasing demand for it, thus driving up its price towards its present value!

Similarly, if the market price were above the present value, then the Consol would be considered "overpriced", and holders of Consols would likely try to sell their holdings. This would increase the supply, driving down the price of the Consol towards its present value.

Whenever players in a market note an opportunity to make a gain from a pricing discrepancy like those above, their actions form a process of "arbitrage", which serves to eliminate the original profitable opportunity by bringing the market back to equilibrium. Ultimately, arbitrage ensures that prices of market-traded assets are "true", in the sense that they match their present value.

There is also the possibility of a perpetuity whose payments (coupons) are growing at a constant rate, g. The present value of such a perpetuity can be calculated using a variant of the above, known as Gordon's growth model:

$$PV = \frac{C}{r - g}$$

This model is discussed more fully in Section 5.6.2, where its application to equity can be seen clearly.

Annuities

An annuity is a contract which provides a series of fixed payments for a given period of time. Thus, an annuity offers the holder a fixed income on a regular basis for a given number of years. It is for this reason that annuities are usually purchased out of the proceeds of an individual's pension fund at the time of retirement, to provide the individual with their pensionable income through their retirement.

Most annuities pay out at the end of each period, and are referred to as an "ordinary annuity" or a "deferred payment annuity". Some annuities, however, pay out at the beginning of each period. These are referred to as an "annuity due". In what follows we shall assume annuities to be ordinary annuities, unless explicitly stated otherwise.

The formula for calculating the present value of an annuity is a variation on the fundamental present value formula. If the regular annuity payment is A for T periods, and the discount rate is r, then the present value of the annuity $PV(A_{r,T})$ is given by:

$$PV\left(A_{r,T}\right) = \sum_{t=1}^{T} \frac{A}{\left(1 + r\right)^t} = A\left[\sum_{t=1}^{T} \frac{1}{\left(1 + r\right)^t}\right]$$

The term in square brackets is often referred to as the "present value interest factor for an annuity" (PVIFA), and can be simplified as follows:

$$PVIFA_{r,T} = \left[\sum_{t=1}^{T} \frac{1}{\left(1 + r\right)^t}\right] = \frac{1 - \dfrac{1}{\left(1 + r\right)^t}}{r}$$

which simplifies to $\dfrac{1}{r} - \dfrac{1}{r\left(1 - r\right)^T}$

A convenient way to consider the present value formula for an annuity is to regard it as equivalent to the difference between the present values on two Consols. An annuity over T years is equivalent to the present value of a Consol with its first payment at the end of the year minus the present value of a Consol whose first payment is at the end of year T. Thus:

$$PV\left(A_{r,T}\right) = \frac{C}{r} - \frac{C}{r}\left[\frac{1}{\left(1 + r\right)^T}\right]$$

Older texts which print PVIF tables will typically also print PVIFA tables as well. A sample of such a PVIFA table is presented below:

Periods (n)	1%	2%	3%	4%	5%	6%	7%	8%
1	0.9901	0.9804	0.9709	0.9615	0.9524	0.9434	0.9346	0.9259
2	1.9704	1.9416	1.9135	1.8861	1.8594	1.8334	1.8080	1.7833
3	2.9410	2.8839	2.8286	2.7751	2.7232	2.6730	2.6243	2.5771
4	3.9020	3.8077	3.7171	3.6299	3.5460	3.4651	3.3872	3.3121
5	4.8534	4.7135	4.5797	4.4518	4.3295	4.2124	4.1002	3.9927
6	5.7955	5.6014	5.4172	5.2421	5.0757	4.9173	4.7665	4.6229
7	6.7282	6.4720	6.2303	6.0021	5.7864	5.5824	5.3893	5.2064
8	7.6517	7.3255	7.0197	6.7327	6.4632	6.2098	5.9713	5.7466
9	8.5660	8.1622	7.7861	7.4353	7.1078	6.8017	6.5152	6.2469
10	9.4713	8.9826	8.5302	8.1109	7.7217	7.3601	7.0236	6.7101
11	10.3676	9.7868	9.2526	8.7605	8.3064	7.8869	7.4987	7.1390
12	11.2551	10.5753	9.9540	9.3851	8.8633	8.3838	7.9427	7.5361

Example:

How much would you be prepared to pay for a five-year annuity offering annual payments of £1,000, given that the appropriate discount rate is 8%?

$$PV\left(A_{r,T}\right) = A\left[\sum_{t=1}^{T}\frac{1}{\left(1+r\right)^{t}}\right]$$

$$PV(A_{8\%,5}) = £1,000\left[\sum_{t=1}^{5}\frac{1}{\left(1+0.08\right)^{t}}\right]$$

$$PV(A_{8\%,5}) = £1,000[3.99271] = £3,992.71$$

The most you would be willing to pay for this annuity is £3,992.71. As with the case of perpetuities, any discrepancy between the price of an annuity in the market and its present value is likely to be eliminated by a process of arbitrage.

3.5.3   The Internal Rate of Return (IRR)

The present value technique offers a useful means for valuation. By bringing future cashflows down to a common denominator—the present value—we have a basis for comparison of cashflows with very different profiles. Present value calculation also allows us to model the value of an asset and compare the outcome with what is on offer in the market. In short, present value is a very useful tool which will allow us to appraise potential investments.

An alternative method of appraising an investment is the Internal Rate of Return (IRR) method. This is especially useful when the discount rate is difficult to determine. The Internal Rate of Return, often labelled by the Greek letter rho (ρ), is best defined as **that discount rate which makes the present value of an investment equal to zero**.

The importance of the IRR is that it offers a single number summarising the merits of an investment. The number depends solely on matters internal to the investment; it is intrinsic to the investment, calculated by internal reference to the cashflows. It does not depend on anything external to the investment. Mathematically, IRR stems from the same formula as present value. The difference is that the discount rate is now the unknown, and we set the NPV to zero. Thus, if C_t represents the net cashflow from the investment during period t:

$$NPV \equiv 0 = \sum_{t=0}^{T} \frac{C_t}{\left(1 + \rho\right)^t}$$

$$NPV \equiv 0 = C_0 + \frac{C_1}{\left(1 + \rho\right)} + \frac{C_2}{\left(1 + \rho\right)^2} + \frac{C_3}{\left(1 + \rho\right)^3} + ... + \frac{C_T}{\left(1 + \rho\right)^T}$$

There are a number of possible methods for solving this equation to find the value of ρ. However, they all ultimately boil down to various forms of "trial and error".

IRR "by hand"
This is the traditional method, employed extensively in the time before personal computers were commonplace. The steps to take are as follows:

1. Arbitrarily select a value for r; 10% is often a good value to begin with. Use this value to calculate the NPV.

2a. If the NPV is greater than zero, then the IRR must be a bigger value. Select a bigger value and recalculate NPV. Go to 2a or 2b as appropriate.

2b. If the NPV is less than zero, the IRR is below the value for r originally selected. Select a smaller value and recalculate NPV. Go to 2a or 2b as appropriate.

Example:

You are offered the opportunity to invest in a project with the following cashflow profile:

C_0	C_1	C_2	C_3
-£1,000	£500	£400	£300

Begin by substituting the cashflows into the equation

$$NPV \equiv 0 = C_0 + \frac{C_1}{(1 + \rho)} + \frac{C_2}{(1 + \rho)^2} + \frac{C_3}{(1 + \rho)^3}$$

to obtain

$$NPV \equiv 0 = -£1,000 + \frac{£500}{(1 + \rho)} + \frac{£400}{(1 + \rho)^2} + \frac{£300}{(1 + \rho)^3}$$

Following step 1, select a trial value for ρ of 10% and calculate:

$$NPV \equiv 0 = -£1,000 + \frac{£500}{(1.1)} + \frac{£400}{(1.1)^2} + \frac{£300}{(1.1)^3}$$

$$NPV = -£1,000 + £454.55 + £330.58 + £225.39$$

$$NPV = -£1,000 + £1,019.72 = £19.72$$

With a positive *NPV* we need to select a higher value for ρ to obtain *NPV* = 0. However, the *NPV* is not greatly above zero, so try 12%:

$$NPV \equiv 0 = -£1,000 + \frac{£500}{(1.12)} + \frac{£400}{(1.12)^2} + \frac{£300}{(1.12)^3}$$

$$NPV = -£1,000 + £446.43 + £318.88 + £213.53 = -£21.16$$

This gives us a negative *NPV*, so the value of ρ which will give *NPV*=0 must lie between the two values we have used so far. Continued trial-and-error of values for ρ between 10% and 12% will ultimately yield the solution (10.65%), but is costly in terms of time, effort and convenience. One alternative is to plot a graph and interpolate:

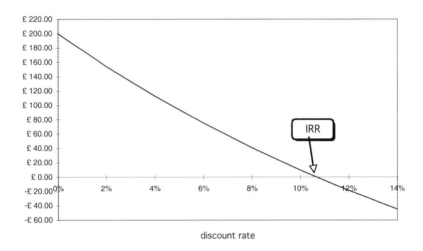

IRR "by computer"
Today, the best alternative is to make use of a spreadsheet application on your personal computer, such as Microsoft® Excel™. The spreadsheet will work via a series of iterations beginning with your first guess as to the value of ρ. The format of the formula entered is

$$= \text{NPV(guess, values)}$$

where "guess" is the starting value for ρ, and "values" refers to the values of the cashflows under consideration. Note that if you do not enter a value for "guess", the software will automatically use a default value of 10%.

While the Internal Rate of Return method has much to commend it, there are a number of drawbacks to its use in many circumstances, which we shall not consider here. In this chapter the focus is on the mechanics of methods of valuation. In Chapter Six we shall consider the application of both IRR and present value techniques to capital budgeting, and also weigh up the relative merits of each method for that purpose.

4. Sources of Finance: Debt

4.1 What is debt?

Debt has a bad name; it has been impugned by such luminaries as William Shakespeare and Charles Dickens! Yet in the modern world there are few people who do not have some form of debt. Debt is simply an obligation or liability to pay—usually money—to someone else. This obligation typically arises because a loan has been taken, and the lender wishes to be paid back on or before a given date, usually with **interest**, a series of payments above the amount lent. But the language can be confusing: someone who has borrowed money is said to be "in debt" (not considered good) or alternatively they can be said to have "acquired credit" (considered good). At its simplest, debt requires the payment of interest and ultimate repayment of **principal** (the amount borrowed), although financial innovation has led to forms of debt where either one of these characteristics is hidden. For example, a zero-coupon bond does not involve the payment of any interest.

The contract of debt is little more than a legal form of IOU, despite appearances to the contrary. Such a contract typically includes details of the borrower, the amount borrowed, and the terms of the loan with regard to frequency of repayments, amount of interest, transferability, security, and any penalties upon default. Yet there is a wide range of different forms of debt in existence. The following describes some of these, and the Appendix to this chapter provides notes on the characteristics of the key major forms of debt.

Bank-originated debt

Most bank-originated debt is typically short- or medium-term in nature. From an individual perspective, the first form of debt we usually encounter is the bank overdraft facility. We are also quite used to the debt we incur via the use of credit cards. Such forms of bank debt are also available to corporate borrowers, who may also incur debt in a large number of other ways. For example, in Chapter Three (Section 3.3.1) we considered the term loan, a loan for a fixed term, for an agreed sum (principal), which may involve both a fee and interest payments. Most term loans incur interest on a floating rate basis plus a margin. Additionally, whereas an overdraft may be secured on all the assets of a company, security for a term loan is normally restricted to the specific assets or the project being financed. One possible alternative to providing security on its own assets is for the company to obtain a guarantee from a third party, such as the parent company if the borrower is a subsidiary.

Trade financing

Trade financing refers primarily to "invoice discounting" or "receivables financing", both forms of factoring whereby a company sells the debts it is owed to a specialised factoring agent usually at a discount, e.g. 80%. The firm then receives immediate money, but less than the full amount of the book debts it has sold. Strictly speaking this is not the same as trade credit, which refers to a situation where a firm pays for commodities it has received after some time has passed. If trade financing occurs on a transnational basis it is often referred to as "forfaiting".

Asset financing

This refers to the raising of funds through the company's existing assets, such as "sale and buy-back" or "sale and lease-back" schemes, or the acquisition of funds for the purchase of a specific asset. This would include leasing of assets as well as hire-purchase agreements.

More specifically, "sale and buy-back" refers to an arrangement in which a company sells an asset, such as land, buildings or equipment, agreeing to repurchase the asset at a specified future date for a given price. Such an arrangement is quite common in financial markets where it is typically referred to as a "repurchase agreement" or "repo". "Sale and lease-back" refers to an arrangement whereby a firm simultaneously sells an asset to another firm (typically to a financial institution) and agrees to lease it back typically for its own long-term use.

Bonds

Sometimes referred to as "loan stock" in the United Kingdom, a bond is a debt contract issued by a company in exchange for the funds which it is borrowing. The bond stipulates the terms of the loan, in terms of time to maturity, interest payments, and principal repayment. The fixed face value of the bond is the redemption value of the bond, and reflects the amount of principal. It is often referred to as the "par" value.

Bonds typically carry a fixed rate of interest, the payment of which is known as the "coupon". The coupon is often set as a percentage of par, although this will not be the same as the yield of the bond, which will vary with market conditions. In UK domestic markets, semi-annual interest payments are common on a 365-day basis. Some bonds carry little or no interest payments, but are offered for sale at a substantial discount. With such "deep discount" or "zero coupon" bonds the incentive to purchase is primarily in the prospect of a capital gain, as the former offer a coupon lower than prevailing market rates while the latter pays no coupon at all.

As with all financial instruments, the yield on offer must adequately reflect the risk involved. Bonds issued by a higher risk corporation must offer the investor a higher rate of return by way of compensation. In a financial system where the markets are efficient, this is ensured via arbitrage. Thus, if a bond considered to be of relatively high risk did not offer enough yield to match investors' expected rates of return, it would fail to find enough buyers. Hence, we would expect to find its price in the market falling, and its yield rising in consequence. A similar consequence would arise in the event of a bond offering a rate of return which exceeded the expectations of investors.

Corporate risk in this context essentially reflects the creditworthiness of the corporate borrower. An entire industry of credit rating agencies has grown up to rate bond issues, particularly in the United States, where the most well-known agencies are Standard & Poor's, Moody's, Duff and Phelps, and Fitch. Standard & Poor's ratings run from AAA down to D, while Moody's system runs from AAa down to C. The following table is illustrative:

Table 4: Bond Rating Categories

S&P	Moody's	
AAA	AAa	Very high quality Ability to repay interest and principal is very strong
AA	AA	
A	A	High quality Slightly more susceptible to changes in economic conditions than higher ratings
BBB	BAA	
BB	Ba	Speculative High risk exposure to adverse conditions
B	B	
CCC	CAA	Very poor
CC	Ca	
C		Reserved for income bonds on which no interest is being paid
D		In default; payment of interest or repayment of principal is in arrears
+ or −		Modifiers for the above categories, to show relative standing within a category

Commentators often make reference to "investment grade" bonds. This refers to bonds which fall within the top four categories of bond rating: for Standard & Poor's this means BBB and above; for Moody's, BAA and higher.

Although a bond can be non-tradable, there is greater incentive for a firm to be able to issue tradable bonds, which will be more attractive to potential lenders due to the increased liquidity. In the United Kingdom, there are two main forms of short- and medium-term debt securities which companies can issue: commercial paper (discussed in Chapter Three; Section 3.3.2) and medium-term notes, which typically have a maturity between one and five years. However, these instruments only apply to listed firms with assets of at least £25 million, and are relatively recent, having been allowed since April 1986.

Long-term debt in the United Kingdom consists primarily of debentures, which are usually secured on the company's assets, unsecured loan stock (sometimes convertible; i.e. with an option to convert to ordinary shares), and preference shares. While banks have traditionally been reluctant to lend long-term in the United Kingdom, there has been some limited quantities of senior debt (which is secured) and mezzanine debt (typically unsecured). Senior debt is repaid by the company before mezzanine debt.

Some loan and bond contracts incorporate a "restrictive covenant", which may serve to constrain the future activities of corporate management. Such restrictions might affect future dividend policy, limit the amount of further borrowing the firm might undertake, or restrict the firm's financial ratios—such as the debt service ratio—within certain ranges.

Some bond contracts also incorporate "call provisions". Less typical nowadays for high credits, these are effectively a form of option which, after a given period of time, enables the company to buy back (i.e. "call") the bond before its date of maturity, for a predetermined amount known as the "call price". The call price is typically at or near its par value. From the firm's perspective, this allows the firm to redeem its debt at an artificially low price if interest rates fall and bond prices rise to the extent that they are above the call price. However, this is extremely unlikely if the market is anywhere near efficient.

4.2   Debt valuation

Bonds of finite maturity
If a debt is in the form of a bond which is traded on a secondary market, then its value will be determined in the same way that the price of any tradable commodities is determined: by the interaction of supply and demand. This will give rise to an equilibrium price for the bond, from which its yield-to-maturity (YTM) can be calculated. This is simply an application of the formula for finding the Internal Rate of Return (IRR). The appropriate variant is:

$$P_B = \sum_{t=1}^{T} \frac{c_t}{(1 + k_d)^t} + \frac{M}{(1 + k_d)^T}$$

where P_B is the current price of the bond, c_t is the coupon payment at time t, M is the maturity value of the bond (i.e., the repayment of principal), and k_d is the yield-to-maturity, which represents the cost of debt capital (hence k_d) to the firm. Note that for most bonds the coupon payment is constant; i.e., $c_t = c_{t+1} = c$, so the bond is an annuity, and the present value of the coupons can be calculated using the formula from Section 3.5.2. Of course, this assumes that the bond has a finite lifespan, at the end of which the bondholder receives M.

This same formula can be used to determine a price for a bond which is not traded in the financial markets. The coupon and par will be known, and the yield on a traded bond with similar characteristics can be used as a proxy for k_d. These values can be substituted into the formula to derive the price of the bond.

Example:

A ten-year bond is paying a coupon of 8 per cent annually on a par of £10,000. If the prevailing yield on bonds of similar risk is 6 per cent, the price of the bond will be given by

$$P_B = \sum_{t=1}^{T} \frac{c_t}{(1 + k_d)^t} + \frac{M}{(1 + k_d)^T}$$

$$P_B = \sum_{t=1}^{10} \frac{(£10,000) * (0.08)}{(1 + 0.06)^t} + \frac{£10,000}{(1 + 0.06)^{10}}$$

$$P_B = \sum_{t=1}^{10} \frac{£800}{(1 + 0.06)^t} + \frac{£10,000}{(1 + 0.06)^{10}}$$

$$P_B = £5,888.07 + £5,583.95 = £11,472.02$$

Note that because the prevailing yield in the market is below the coupon, the bond is selling at a premium ($P_B >$ par). It follows logically that there is an inverse relationship between bond yields and bond prices: when yields fall, prices rise, and *vice versa*. It is worth noting that the coupon payment is fixed; it is the prevailing yield which adjusts to reflect market conditions.

Bonds of infinite maturity
For bonds of infinite maturity ("perpetuities") the formula above reduces to:

$$P_B = \frac{c}{r}$$

In Chapter Three we discussed Consols as an example of a perpetuity. Since 1991, the only other example of perpetual debt in the UK has been the issue of Permanent Interest-Bearing Shares (PIBS) by several building societies. The mutual nature of many building societies means that PIBS are as close as you can get to holding equity in some building societies. PIBS are fixed interest securities with no redemption date. While there is a (perpetual) stream of regular coupon payments, the investment can only be realised by selling the PIBS on the open market (the London Stock Exchange), and making a capital gain or loss. However, the market for PIBS is relatively small, and it is not always easy to find a buyer (or seller). Because of this, PIBS need to offer a relatively high yield to make them attractive to investors.

Example:

> Consider a Consol with a 4% coupon. Current market yields are at 8.56%. Given that Consols are usually quoted in the *Financial* Times in units of £100 nominal value, with the price in pounds and fractions (usually thirty-seconds) of a pound, what price would you be prepared to pay?
>
> $$P_B = \frac{c}{r} = \frac{0.04}{0.0856}$$
>
> $$P_B = (£100)^*(0.4673) = £46.73 = £46\frac{23}{32}$$

4.3   Not-quite-debt: hybrids

Convertibles
A convertible bond has all the characteristics of any other bond, with the added attraction that it offers the holder the opportunity within a given time frame to exchange the bonds for ordinary shares. The bondholder may be required to pay a conversion fee.

The value of a convertible bond will always be at least equal to the value of a non-convertible bond with otherwise identical characteristics.

In most cases, the value of the convertible will exceed that of its non-convertible "twin" as it is essentially a combination of the non-convertible bond and a call option on the company's ordinary shares. Consequently, the value of the convertible bond should equal the value of its non-convertible twin plus the value of the call option. By way of corollary, this means that the yield on a convertible bond will be less than that on its non-convertible twin.

Warrants

Similar to convertibles in many ways are warrants. These do not offer the warrant holder the right to exchange bonds for equity, but are effectively a self-contained option (written by the company) to purchase a quantity of the company's equity at a predetermined price (the "exercise price"). The warrant is issued as a complement to the bond. If the warrant is exercised the holder still has his existing bonds intact, as well as the newly-acquired ordinary shares. Because of the separability, a warrant is typically a cheaper form of finance than an equivalent convertible bond.

4.4   Interest rate determination

In the foregoing we have examined the institutional aspects of debt financing, as well as some valuation models. The key to understanding debt fully is to understand what underpins the price of debt, **interest**.

All economic exchanges—whether barter or monetary—can be categorised according to the timing of the two sides of the trade:

spot transaction: a trade in which both sides of the transaction occur simultaneously.

credit transaction: a trade in which goods are supplied now in return for payment in the future.

forward transaction: a trade in which a current payment is made for goods to be supplied in the future.

In order for a credit or forward transaction to be feasible, some additional incentive beyond the normal gains from trade is required. This incentive normally takes the form of the payment of interest. Interest may properly be regarded as the price of credit (loanable funds, or debt). Like the price of any other marketable commodity, the rate of interest will normally be determined by the interaction of supply and demand:

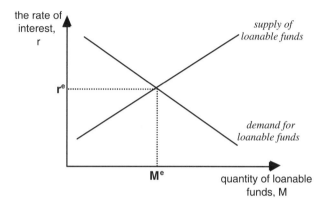

In one sense, we may think of the rate of interest as rent paid for the (temporary) use of other people's money. That would be consistent with a dictionary definition of interest. But there is more to interest than a "pure rental rate of money". There is also the need for interest to include some form of compensation for risk. Five risk categories may be identified:

1. **Default risk**: this concerns the likelihood that the issuer of a security will fail to honour their obligation. Security issuers with a long history of punctually meeting their obligations are likely to be less risky than those issued by less reputable characters. The amount of default risk may also be influenced (positively) by the period to maturity of a security; the longer to maturity, the greater the default risk.

2. **Purchasing power risk**: this relates to uncertainty about the purchasing power of the unit of currency, and occurs as a result of inflation (or deflation). Because interest is usually expressed in nominal terms, the security's real rate of interest will depend upon movements in the general price level. This is represented in the well-known "Fisher equation"

$$R_{real} = R_{nominal} - \Pi$$

where R represents the rate of interest (with the appropriate subscript) and Π represents the (expected) rate of inflation. Equally, the greater the volatility of the rate of inflation the more purchasing power risk is assumed.

3. **Marketability risk**: this depends upon the likelihood that a security can be realised (sold) without much danger of loss, and relates directly to the existence and efficiency of any secondary markets. Similarly, following Silber [1970], this category should explicitly include:

    > ...factors such as imperfect knowledge on behalf of participants in the secondary market or the existence of only a small number of traders in the market account for the fact that an attempt to sell a large block of the security requires a significant decrease in price... (page 8)

    Marketability risk is sometimes referred to as reversibility risk, because it relates to the ability of the investor to reverse their decision.

4. **Capital value risk**: this arises because there may be uncertainty attached to the security of the principal. The greater the likelihood of the market value of any security fluctuating over time, the greater the degree of capital value risk involved. Ryan [1978] suggests that this kind of risk is especially likely if an investor's assets have longer to go to maturity than his liabilities.

5. **Income risk**: according to Clayton and Osborn [1965] this occurs because "interest income cannot be predicted with certainty beyond the maturity and call dates of a security". Ryan [1978] suggests this type of risk to be most likely when an investor's assets have a shorter maturity horizon than his liabilities.

We may therefore identify the key components which make up the nominal rate of interest:

- A "pure rental rate of money" to compensate the lender for the opportunity cost. Because this component involves no payment for risk it is also referred to as the "risk-free" rate of interest

- An inflation risk premium to compensate the lender for possible losses of purchasing power
- Other risk premiums to compensate for the other kinds of risk considered above

In addition, interest may also include an implicit profit margin (for the lender). This margin often appears as the "spread" between borrowing rates and lending rates, and is particularly noticeable at the high street banks. How large this spread is depends upon the current state of competitiveness in the financial markets. The greater the competition, the smaller the spread.

Taken together we see that the rate of interest consists of a "risk-free" rate plus the five risk premia noted above. However, it is not possible in practice to determine the proportions of a given rate of interest accounted for by the individual risk premia.

4.5   The Term Structure of Interest Rates

Economists, particularly macroeconomists, have a tendency to talk about "the rate of interest", despite the fact that there is a whole spectrum of interest rates in existence. This is not attributable to any myopia on the part of economists; rather it is a conversational convenience that stems from the fact that interest rates largely have a tendency to move together. When taking a less broad view of economic affairs, such as analysing financial markets, the nature of the spectrum of interest rates is explicitly considered under the heading of the Term Structure of Interest Rates.

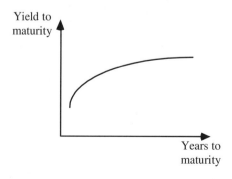

The Term Structure of Interest Rates refers to the relationship between the yields obtainable on similar securities of differing maturity. The yield curve (illustrated above) is a graphical representation of the relationship between similar securities of differing maturity and their yields (rates of interest).

Intuitively, an upward-sloping yield curve like that depicted is expected, and is also commonly experienced. Nonetheless, it is entirely feasible to find a downward-sloping yield curve, a U-shaped yield curve, or even one which is humped (inverted U).

Several competing theories have been put forward to account for the yield curve, as well as a substantial body of empirical work, yet there is still little consensus regarding their validity. Nonetheless, the shape of the yield curve does seem to change in a stable, predictable manner as the economy moves through the various stages of the business cycle. A "good" theory of the Term Structure of Interest Rates must account for both its shape and its movement over time. Arguably the most intuitively plausible theory offering an explanation for the yield curve is based on the notion that the difference between short- and long-term yields is due entirely to expectations.

4.5.1   The Expectations Hypothesis

The origins of this Hypothesis are to be found in John Hicks' 1946 classic, *Value and Capital*. Put simply, the Expectations Hypothesis posits that long-term rates of interest are an average of expected short-term rates of interest. That is to say, expectations play a predominant role in determining interest rates. Because this relationship depends on the existence and widespread use of arbitrage—and by implication, the existence of efficient markets (see Chapter Two, Section 2.2.2)—it has a widespread intuitive appeal, particularly for theoretical economists.

The major premise underlying the Expectations Hypothesis is that bonds of differing maturities are close (or at best, "perfect") substitutes. For example, suppose investors have a choice between putting their funds into a two-year bond offering a rate of interest of R per annum, or buying a one-year bond for the current year paying r_1 and then placing the proceeds during the second year into a further one-year bond which is expected to be paying r_2. The existence of arbitrage then means that:

$$(1 + R)^2 = (1 + r_1)(1 + r_2)$$

In other words, in equilibrium the yield on a two-year bond and two one-year bonds will be equivalent. To see that this must be the case, consider what would happen if (say) the two-year bond offered a greater return than the two one-year bonds:

$$(1 + R)^2 > (1 + r_1)(1 + r_2)$$

In this case, there would be little incentive for the rational investor to purchase the two one-year bonds. Investors would therefore seek to place their funds in the higher-yielding two-year bond. Consequently, we would observe increased demand for two-year bonds, leading to an increase in their price, and consequently a decline in their yield, R. Equally, there would be a decline in demand for the one-year bonds, lowering their prices, and raising their yields, r_1 and r_2. This process—**arbitrage**—will continue until equilibrium is achieved, as shown in the first equation above.

More generally, we can extrapolate from above to determine that the yield on a long-term bond is an average of expected (spot) yields on short-term bonds. Letting $_er_t$ represent the (expected) yield on a single-year bond held during year t, we obtain:

$$(1 + R)^T = (1 + _er_1)(1 + _er_2)(1 + _er_3)...(1 + _er_T)$$

Under the Expectations Hypothesis it follows that forward rates of interest should be equal to the expected future (spot) rates. It therefore follows that any attempt to validate empirically the Expectations Hypothesis must concentrate on testing forward rates as predictors of future spot rates.

The kind of yield curve implied by the Expectations Hypothesis depends on the interest rate expectations held by market participants. If short-term rates of interest were expected to rise, we would expect to find an upward-sloping yield curve (as previously illustrated). Expected declining short-term rates imply a downward sloping yield curve. A period of rising expected short-term rates followed by a decline in expected short-term rates implies a "humped" yield curve. Thus, the Expectations Hypothesis offers a plausible explanation for a yield curve of any shape. Its primary weakness is that it offers no real explanation for shifts in the position of the yield curve.

4.5.2   Liquidity Preference

The Expectations Hypothesis is largely grounded in the notion that there will be "investors" who will act to bring about equilibrium through arbitrage. This theory of the term structure of interest rates has its origins in the work of Keynes [1936], who put forward the theory of Liquidity Preference as an explanation of the demand for money. It is also to be found in Hicks [1946], who may be regarded as treating the term structure as being determined jointly by liquidity preference and expectations. Thus, Liquidity Preference theory is regarded by many as an extension or modification of the Expectations Hypothesis. It is based primarily on the premise that, as a result of risk aversion, there is a liquidity risk premium positively associated with a security's maturity: the longer a security has before it matures, the greater the liquidity premium that investors will require to compensate them for the additional risk. Thus, the actual forward rate must exceed the expected short-rate by a risk-premium to compensate for the loss of liquidity. Equilibrium occurs when:

$$(1 + R)^T = (1 + {}_1r_1 + \lambda_1)\,(1 + {}_1r_2 + \lambda_2)\,(1 + {}_1r_3 + \lambda_3) \dots (1 + {}_1r_T + \lambda_T)$$

where ${}_1r_t$ represents the currently (period 1) expected (spot) rate of interest in period t, and $\lambda_1 < \lambda_2 < \lambda_3 < \dots < \lambda_T$ represent the monotonically-increasing liquidity risk premiums for the relevant time-periods, 1 through T.

One consequence of this theory is that forward rates may not equal expected future (spot) rates, the difference being the liquidity risk premium. While there have been many attempts to empirically compare the Expectations Hypothesis with the Liquidity Preference theory, according to Kolb [1985]:

> The conflict between these two theories has yet to be resolved. If there is a liquidity premium, causing forward rates and expected future spot rates to diverge, it is probably quite small. At any rate, both parties agree that forward rates are intimately related to expected future spot rates.   (page 140)

The yield curve implied by the Liquidity Preference once again depends on the interest rate expectations held by market participants, and to what degree they enhance or offset the effect of the liquidity premiums. The existence of monotonically-increasing liquidity premiums makes an upward-sloping yield curve more likely than under the Expectations Hypothesis, however. Liquidity Preference offers a plausible explanation for a yield curve of any shape, while suggesting that there is a greater likelihood of it being upward sloping. Like the Expectations Hypothesis, the primary weakness of the Liquidity Preference explanation is that it offers no real explanation for shifts in the position of the yield curve.

4.5.3   Hedging pressure/Preferred habitat/Market segmentation

A range of alternative theories of the Term Structure of Interest Rates to the Expectations Hypothesis and Liquidity Preference theory is grounded in the ideas of Jack Culbertson [1957]. Based on his empirical testing of the Expectations Hypothesis, Culbertson concluded:

> ...the explanation of broad movements in the term structure of interest rates must be sought principally in factors other than behavior governed by interest rate expectations.   (page 502)

Culbertson's ideas stem from the notion that similar securities of different maturity are not good substitutes for one another. Because of this the markets for loans of different maturities are largely "segmented". What happens in the market for short-term assets has little or no relationship to occurrences in the market for medium- or long-term assets. Yields on assets with short-term maturities can be either greater or less than yields on assets of longer maturities, depending entirely on the independent supply and demand conditions prevailing in each of those separate markets.

This segmentation may occur in large part due to the increasing dominance of the financial markets by the large institutional investors, such as life insurance companies and pension funds. According to the theory of financial intermediation, institutions will tend to hedge; thus, if an institution's liabilities are predominantly long-term, the assets they choose to hold will also tend to be long-term. Such institutions will find little in maturity switching to commend it to them. Thus, they may be said to have a "preferred habitat", a maturity range of the market in which they prefer to operate, regarding other maturity ranges as poor substitutes.

In its strongest form, this theory suggests that investors will tend to operate exclusively within a maturity range, regardless of possible arbitrage profits that might be made by maturity switching along the lines expressed in the Expectations Hypothesis. Under this scenario, markets will be segmented strictly with participants at one part of the yield curve not straying to participate elsewhere on the curve.

In a weaker, looser form, while investors may have a preferred habitat, due to the requirements of hedging, under certain (exceptional) circumstances they may be persuaded to switch to a different maturity range to take advantage of possible arbitrage profits, at least temporarily. This certainly would seem to be the case for UK pension funds, who tend to hold small, relatively insignificant fractions (less than 4%) of their portfolio holdings in liquid assets, preferring ordinary shares and long-term bonds in particular. Yet following the oil crisis of the early 1970s, they dramatically increased their holding of liquid assets to nearly 17% of total holdings.

In his empirical study of the market for government securities, Michaelsen [1965] found support for the role of expectations as well as for market segmentation. He notes

> It would appear that most portfolios, and especially those of large institutional holders, have indeterminate rather than fixed liquidation dates, their maturity composition remaining roughly constant over time or changing in response to forces other than the passage of time.   (page 461)

Malkiel [1966] took a more institutional view, which came to represent the hedging pressure approach. He concluded:

> The bond market is not segmented in any absolute manner. ...we found that most investors substituted broadly among securities over wide ranges of the yield curve in accordance with their expectations ... [yet] strong maturity preferences are present in both sides of the market. A valid version ... asserts simply that many buyers and sellers must be paid differentiated premiums to induce them to move from their preferred maturities.

Weaker versions, under the aegis of preferred habitat theories, have sought to integrate market segmentation with expectations, including the work of Modigliani and Sutch [1967]. According to McCallum [1975] these attempts are:

> ...characterized by a multiple horizon market and a willingness on the part of investors to acquire non-horizon instruments within a range called a habitat. It is argued that the existence of habitats gives the market a continuity which is not present in the segmentation theory. (page 307)

4.5.4 Clientele effect

More recent attempts to explain the yield curve have tried to take into account institutional factors. The clientele effect considers the effect of taxation on the yield curve, and may be regarded as an extension of the preferred habitat idea. It is grounded in the fact that there may be different tax classes of investors whose habitat on the yield curve is determined by their tax class. Of particular relevance is the distinction between tax on interest and tax on capital growth, which may affect investor preference for different maturities of bond.

4.5.5 Afterthoughts

It should be readily apparent from the foregoing that there is little consensus among economists with regard to explanations of the term structure of interest rates. According to David Laidler [1985]:

> The most satisfactory theory of the term structure appears to be one that rests on the proposition that (with suitable adjustment for risk) expected holding-period yields on assets of various maturities tend to be equalized by the market. ... This expected holding-period yield, of course, includes capital gains and losses made over the period. (page 91)

Nonetheless, lack of consensus does not imply a lack of validity. Indeed, empirical evidence suggests that each theory has some validity during specific economic conditions: Liquidity Preference seems to work well when interest rates are expected to remain relatively stable; when interest rates are generally high, and expected to fall, the expectations hypothesis seems to be valid; and there is mixed evidence on the market segmentation view.

There have been many attempts to bring together elements from each of the foregoing into a "grand unified theory" of the term structure. These attempts have been quite technical and have yet to offer us greater insight than the basic theories outlined above. For example, more recent work has tended to build on the work of Cox, Ingersoll and Ross [1981, 1985] in recognising that there are many factors which shape the yield curve. Their model attempts to encompass all the elements of previous theories—such as those outlined in this chapter—in a manner that is consistent with maximising behaviour and rational expectations.

Finally, it is worth noting that central banks, such as the Bank of England, (or the government if the central bank is not independent) often focus their policy on an interest rate target as a means of controlling economic activity. This may act to distort interest rates in the short-run. In terms of the yield curve this means that central bank activity tends to operate on the short end of the market.

Appendix: Notes on Debt Sources

This Appendix offers brief pointers to the main characteristics of the various forms in which corporate debt manifests itself. This list is meant to be illustrative, rather than fully inclusive.

Short- and Medium-Term Debt

1. *Overdraft facilities*
   - borrower can borrow up to an agreed amount at will (very informal)
   - repayable on demand
   - market-related interest (percentage above bank's base lending rate)
   - fee possible
   - security is usually both a fixed (on premises or given assets) and floating charge (on remaining assets)

2. *Term loans*
   - formal agreement, normally from 2–5 years
   - possible "grace period" (no principal repayments during the early life of the loan; e.g., for 2 years on a five-year loan)
   - equal periodic payments; some possibility of flexible repayments, so "bullet" or "balloon" payments and prepayments possible
   - market-related interest (percentage over LIBOR)
   - arrangement fee normally involved
   - security usually on specific assets; third-party guarantees possible
   - covenanting on ratio compliance: debt/equity, current ratio

3. *Guarantee facilities*
   - refers to third-party guarantee arranged for a fee by the bank
   - used to establish relationship with other lender(s) with access to low-cost financing (usually for specific purposes)

4. *Multiple option facilities (MOFs)*
    - a combination facility: such as term loans and overdraft
    - may require third-party guarantees, letters of credit, etc.

5. *Syndicated facilities*
    - refers to where a single borrower deals with many lenders (in syndicate)

6. *Asset financing*
    - leasing and hire purchase: allows use of an asset financed by another party
    - sale and lease-back/buy-back

7. *Trade financing*
    - factoring: purchase by specialist of trade debts
    - invoice discounting/receivables financing
    - forfaiting: usually implies cross-border transaction

8. *Revolving underwriting facility (RUF)*
    - international source, started in early 1980s
    - issue of short-term paper under a medium-term underwriting commitment
    - an institution—such as a bank—underwrites fund access at specified rate (normally linked to LIBOR)

9. *Trade credit*
    - deferred payment/discount

10. *Bills of Exchange*
    - mainly used in international transactions
    - approximately equivalent to a post-dated cheque
    - "an unconditional order in writing, addressed by one person to another, signed by the person giving it, requiring the person to whom it is addressed to pay on demand, or at a fixed or determinable future time, a sum certain in money to or to the order of a specified person, or to bearer"
                          (Bills of Exchange Act 1882, section 3)

11. *Acceptance credit facilities*
    - raising funds by discounting of Bills of Exchange

12. *Deferred tax payments*

13. *Medium-term bank loans*
    - available since 1970s
    - usually 1–5 years
    - repayments: lump-sum / periodic…
    - normally variable interest: 2–5% over bank base rate
    - arrangement fee
    - security—fixed or floating charge
    - covenant

14. *Government-guaranteed loans*
    - available since 1981
    - government guarantees 70% to banker in event of default
    - possibility of moral hazard (for example because of the government guarantee, a lender might be inclined to offer loans to clients which they would otherwise deem lacking in creditworthiness)

15. *Merchant bank financing*
    - primarily the provision of risk or venture capital
    - loans are typically for more than £250,000

16. *Investors in Industry (3i)*
    - parent company of Industrial and Commercial Finance Corporation (ICFC)
    - formed in 1983 to provide finance (through loans and equity capital) for small- and medium-sized enterprises (SMEs)
    - original ownership: 85% by clearing banks, 15% by Bank of England. Listed on the London Stock Exchange

17. *Export finance: primary sources*
    - overdrafts
    - short-term fixed-interest loans
    - discounted Bills of Exchange
    - acceptance credits
    - Export Credits Guarantee Department (ECGD)

18. *Debt security issue*
    - direct financing—avoids banking sector (typically lower costs)

- originally unavailable due to Banking Act 1979, restricting short-term fund access without Bank of England authority
- Banking Act 1987: allowed for development of sterling commercial paper (CP) market
- Conditions for issuing debt securities:
    (a) net assets of at least £25m, and shares or debt traded/listed
    (b) debt securities issues, transferable in minimum amounts of £100,000
    (c) maturity: CP 7 days–1 year; medium-term notes 1–5 years

Long-Term Debt

1. *Bank (and other institutional) loans*
    - term loans
    - interest—fixed, floating; around 3–6% over bank base rate
    - arrangement fee: normally around 1%
    - security—property, assets ("senior debt")
    - sometimes unsecured ("meClemenceanine debt")

2. *Debentures*
    - also known as "loan stock" (in USA debentures refers to unsecured loan stock)
    - usually secured via trust deed, so there is a prior floating charge on the company assets
    - mortgage debenture is a debenture secured on property

3. *Unsecured loan stock*
    - unsecured, so yield higher than on debentures
    - covenants usual

4. *Preference shares*
    - considered debt/equity hybrid, with many varieties
    - typically involves some form of ownership
    - periodic payment known as a "dividend"
    - rank after debt in claims on the company
    - yield higher than that on unsecured debt securities

5. Sources of Finance: Equity

5.1 What Is Equity?

In considering the provision of funds to a company there are two basic possibilities. The first is to lend money to the company, and receive a return regardless of how well the company is performing. The second possibility is to pay for a "piece of the action", to use the vernacular. This implies putting money into the company and receiving a share of the profits. By so doing it is implied that you will also have some say as to how the company is run. This latter method illustrates equity funding. The holder of debt has a legal right to be repaid. This is not the case for the holder of equity. Thus, for the provider of funds, equity is considered more risky and would therefore be expected to generate a higher rate of return.

For many people the phrase "equity" is often commensurate with "ordinary shares". The word itself comes from the root "equals", implying that any individual share in the company is identically equal to any other share in the company (of the same class). Equity involves part-ownership of the company, according to the number of shares held by the investor. The equity-holder—or shareholder—is therefore a part-owner of the company, and thus entitled to participatory rights. These normally include

- voting entitlement
- dividend participation
- return of capital in the event of the firm's liquidation.

5.1.1 Types of share capital
While equity can refer to any kind of ownership, including that in property, in the corporate context there are two primary forms: ordinary shares, and preference shares. For the general public, "shares" are

synonymous with stock exchange activities, but this is only true for companies with a stock exchange listing, which are those with a very large capitalisation. Far and away, the largest number of companies are private limited companies (denoted by the term "limited" in their title). Listed companies are a subset of public limited companies (denoted by "plc"). However, under the various Companies Acts, all limited liability companies are able to issue shares, as discussed in Chapter One.

5.2 Ordinary Shares (or Stock)

This is the basic equity investment within a company. Every company must start its life with an issue of ordinary shares, which represents the ultimate ownership of the company. Shareholders normally receive a certificate indicating their (part-) ownership; however, the rights and obligations of shareholders are normally defined within the company's Articles of Association. Ordinary shares—known as "common stock" in the United States—typically possess one vote per share. It is feasible to have various classes of ordinary shares with different voting rights, but this is not welcomed by professional investors. Consequently, there has been a general convergence towards a single class of ordinary shares, particularly for listed companies.

Because they are part-owners of the company, ordinary shareholders have voting rights in accordance with the Articles and Memorandum of Association. Shareholders vote for a Board of Directors to act as their representatives ("agents"). Such votes normally occur at the company's Annual General Meeting. At the AGM shareholders also (effectively) appoint the auditors who, as representatives of the shareholders, are required to check the periodic reports produced by the Board of Directors for shareholders. The Board is expected to deal with the company's senior management on a regular basis.

As the shareholders are the owners of the company, they own any profits. Any portion of the profits which is distributed to shareholders comes in the form of a **dividend**. Ordinary shareholders have no automatic entitlement to a dividend, but usually vote on them at the AGM based on the Board's recommendation. Dividends can only be paid out of current or retained earnings. In the event of liquidation, shareholders are paid out after all other prior claims have been met from the assets of the business. Shareholders have full rights to the remainder.

5.3   Preference Shares

The popularity of preference shares, a source of long-term finance, declined considerably in the UK following the changes in the system of corporation tax introduced in 1966. At that time, many companies converted their existing preference shares into debentures.

Legally, preference shares (known as "preferred stock" in the USA) cannot be the only form of equity within a company, although they may feasibly represent the majority of equity capital. In common with ordinary shares, preference shares pay a dividend, which consequently is not a right, but based on the recommendation of the Board. Nonetheless, preference shares are typically non-participatory and thus are not always regarded as equity, being seen as having characteristics closer to those of debt.

Preference shares have priority over ordinary shares in the payment of dividend, and hence they often pay dividends at a pre-defined rate. This rate may be fixed or adjustable (for example, against some floating interest rate). **Participating** preference shares permit the holder to a share in the firm's earnings over and above the pre-defined rate. Note that preference shares are usually issued as **cumulative** preference shares. In this case, any shortfall in dividend that may occur is accumulated and must be paid in full before ordinary shareholders can receive any dividend.

In the event of liquidation, preference shareholders are usually paid out to the face value of the preference shares before ordinary shareholders, but after debtholders. Preference shareholders have no further claims on the company. Preference shares are generally redeemable, but only from fresh capital or retained earnings. They may also be "puttable", in that the holders may have the right to insist upon redemption at a predetermined rate on certain dates.

Preference shares may be issued on a **convertible** basis, whereby they can be converted into ordinary shares at a predetermined rate and on specific dates, but at the option of the preference shareholder.

By their very nature, preference shares are considered less risky than ordinary shares and consequently have a lower expected return. Convertible preference shares are often issued as "mezzanine finance" to venture capitalists. If the company is doing well the preference shares will be converted into ordinary shares, whereas if the firm performs badly a fixed return is received until such time as there is improvement or the company is liquidated.

5.4   Other Points of Note

In addition to the main types of equity there are also equity-related instruments referred to as "hybrids", as they possess characteristics of both debt and equity.

As we have seen in Chapter Four, convertible debt securities are issued as straight debt having a par value, paying interest and with a known maturity. However, after a period of time they are convertible into ordinary shares at a predetermined rate at the holder's option. Conversion rights are generally protected against dilution due to the issue of more shares.

The existence of conversion rights on corporate bonds is generally to act as an inducement—a "sweetener"—to ensure sufficient investor demand. The conversion option is considered valuable in itself, so that convertibles offer a lower coupon (interest payments) than straight debt of similar characteristics. If the company is perceived as successful, then investors may value the conversion rights highly, in which case they may be prepared to accept lower interest payments in the meantime.

"Zero-coupon convertibles" were a preferred method of funding for a number of high-flying property and asset-stripping companies in the 1970s. The bonds often possess "put" (see above) and "call" provisions, giving the company the right to redeem the bonds on certain dates if (for example) interest rates drop significantly from the date of issue.

An equity "warrant" offers a long-dated option to purchase a predetermined number of shares at a predetermined price (or prices) at a certain time (or times) in the future. These are often issued as sweeteners, attached to ordinary bonds to reduce the coupon rate. Typically the option dates are measured in years, although it is feasible to find perpetual warrants. These would normally possess call features.

5.5   Raising Equity Capital

When a company is first founded it raises ordinary equity capital. This is money provided by the original shareholders in exchange for ordinary shares. For a small company registering for limited liability at Companies House, there must be at least one director and a company secretary (not the same person as the director) or two directors, who must take up at least two shares of the company. Small limited companies typically begin with a minimum authorised (or nominal) share capital of £100. This amount is stated in the Memorandum of Association, and refers to the limit to which the company is authorised shares. Thus, a company with shares at a par (face value) of £1 and a nominal share capital of £100 can issue up to 100 shares. If the par was 50p, then 200 shares is the maximum which can be issued. The par value of the shares actually issued is referred to as the "issued capital". It is entirely feasible for the shares to be sold for an amount in excess of par. This excess is known as the "share premium". A public limited company (plc) must have authorised capital of at least £50,000, with at least 25% of the issued share capital's nominal value plus any premium being paid.

Some companies may decide that the shares they issue do not need to be paid for in full at the time of issue. Part-payment is taken on issue, with the remainder being collected at a later date. "Paid-up capital" is the amount actually collected upon issue, the shares being referred to as "partly paid". "Uncalled capital" refers to the unpaid value of the issued shares.

Example:

Consider a company with authorised share capital of £1,000 divided into 1,000 shares at £1. If the company issues 100 shares partly-paid at 25p each, it will have a paid-up share capital of (100)*(25p) = £25.00

Uncalled capital for each share issued is 75p, or (100)*(75p) = £75.00 in total.

Example: (premiums)

> A public company allots £1 shares at £2 per share. The premium per
> share is thus £1, while the nominal value is £1. The company must collect
> on issue £1.25 per share, made up of the £1 premium per share, and 25%
> of the nominal value.

As a company grows and becomes successful in its operations it will
require additional funding, for expansion or other investment, for example,
or even to repay some debt. It may first try to raise more capital through
debt or preference shares. Alternatively, a company might try to raise
further funds through an issue of further equity, known as a **rights issue**.

Success occurs when the firm finds holders for its newly-issued
shares who are willing to pay the asking price. While there is no fixed
cost to the shares, potential holders of the new shares would expect to
share in the earnings and dividends of the company in perpetuity with the
holders of existing shares. Thus, the expectation is that money previously
available for distribution to the holders of existing shares will be
reduced; their pre-existing holding is said to have become "diluted", and
their degree of participation is diminished. Because of this adverse effect
it is customary to offer the new shares in the first instance to existing
shareholders in proportion to their existing holdings. Only those not
taken up by existing shareholders can then be offered to new investors.
Known as "pre-emptive rights", this is a legal requirement when raising
additional equity funding in many countries, including the United
Kingdom. It should be quite apparent that a rights issue is likely to be
more successful for a listed company than for a private limited company.
If a rights issue is successful, then the amount raised would be

$$(\text{number of shares}) * (\text{issue price}) - (\text{expenses})$$

where expenses can typically range anywhere between 2% and 5%.

Example:

> A company has an existing issued equity capital of 1,000,000 shares at a
> par of 25p. The current share price is 200p. The company wishes to raise
> £375,000, which is a substantial increase on the company's current
> market capitalisation of (200p)*(1,000,000) = £2,000,000.

The company believes that if it offers the new shares near the current market price it is unlikely to find many subscribers (investors) taking up the offer due to the possible dilution effect. Therefore, it decides to offer them at a discount, at a price of 150p each. Assuming expenses to be zero (for simplicity), this would mean offering (£375,000/£1.50) = 250,000 shares. Thus, each shareholder would be given the opportunity to buy one new share for each of the four old ones they owned—a "one-for-four" rights issue.

If a shareholder takes up the rights, then the value of their holding will be

$$(4 * 200p) + (1 * 150p) = 950p$$

Thus, 950p represents the value of 5 shares, giving an "ex-rights" price of 190p per share. Theoretically, this should be the price the shares will trade for in the market following the issue.

Suppose an individual shareholder declined to take up his rights, thereby diluting his stake in the company. The value of his holding would decline by 10p per share. Hence, if he does not want to take up the rights, he should sell them for 40p per new share, or else he will find his wealth diminished by 10p per share he holds. The mechanics of this are straightforward: shareholders usually receive an allotment letter for the new shares in proportion to their existing holding; this letter may be sold on to a third party.

Note that this example makes no assumption about any additional earnings the company might be able to make using of the additional capital raised.

It is up to the directors to decide the appropriate ratio in which to issue the new shares, after taking advice from various quarters. Suppose in the example above the directors believed, for one reason or another, that the current share price to be too high, and thus a disincentive to potential investors. One possibility would be to offer a "two-for-one" rights issue. This would imply 500,000 new shares, and hence a price of 75p each. The ex-rights price would be 158.3p

If the directors decided the share price was too high but did not wish to raise more capital then a common solution would be a "scrip issue".

This means issuing more shares, but giving them to existing shareholders in proportion to their current holding. A "two-for-one" scrip issue would mean issuing 500,000 new shares; the ex-scrip price would be $(200p)*(1m/1.5m) = 133p$.

As we have seen, when a company is originally incorporated its shares are often "taken up" (bought) by people directly involved in the management of the company. As the firm grows, subsequent rights issues may prove too onerous for the original shareholders, so steps are taken to increase the number of shareholders. One way of doing this is by means of a rights issue, but with existing shareholders electing not to take up their rights, preferring to sell them in a concerted fashion to selected financial institutions, for example. This is known as a "private placement" of equity.

Unlike a private limited company, a public company can sell its shares directly to the public. The simplest way to do this would be in an appropriate public environment. Thus, another common way of enlarging the circle of shareholders is to obtain a listing on a stock exchange of some form. A stock exchange provides a marketplace for the shares of the company, so that anybody may purchase or sell them. Listing is, however, subject to certain stringent conditions being met. For example:

- the exchange has to be provided with information about the company—such as its history, details about its management, and about its profitability—so that prospective buyers may know something about the company;
- there must be a minimum amount of shares available for purchase or sale on the exchange. The main market of the London International Stock Exchange (LSE) requires at least 25% of the equity capital to be available ("in public hands"). London's Alternative Investment Market, AIM ("our global market for young and growing companies") has no minimum requirement for shares in public hands. Interestingly, AIM's predecessor, the Unlisted Securities Market (USM) required 10%.

If a company grows and to the extent that it finds a single exchange does not provide it with a sufficient range of investors, then it may seek to be "introduced" on another stock exchange, possibly in another country. Because exchanges have different rules—known as "listing requirements"—that must be satisfied before quotation, it may become immensely time-consuming and costly for a company to comply with the information disclosure rules of a number of exchanges. This is particularly true of US exchanges, whose rules are considered by some to be onerous. For example, quarterly reporting is the norm in the USA, while semi-annual reporting occurs in the UK. Accounting disclosure standards are also much higher in the USA than (for example) Germany, which requires little information to be passed to shareholders. As a result, to-date very few German companies have sought a US listing, although German companies in particular increasingly view the benefits of a US listing outweighing the extra disclosure costs. It is interesting to note that the first German company to gain a US listing was Daimler-Benz (now part of Daimler-Chrysler). In March 2004, there were three German companies listed on the New York Stock Exchange, with another 14 listed via ADRs.

"American Depository Receipts" (ADRs) provide an alternative to a direct listing in the USA. Suppose a UK company deposits sterling-denominated UK-listed shares with a US bank. In turn, the bank sells to US investors dollar-denominated tradeable securities called ADRs, which represent the underlying UK shares. US regulation is such that the ADR has to be registered with the US Securities and Exchange Commission (SEC). The American purchaser of the ADR possesses all the rights and benefits of a UK shareholder, but not the rights and benefits of an owner of a US-listed share. The bank is usually responsible for the handling of aspects of the UK share, such as dividends and rights issues. Because the ADR concept has been quite successful, it has extended to International or Global ADRs, which effectively allow shares to be traded around the world.

5.6   Equity Valuation

Any company whose shares are listed on a stock market will find the price of those shares determined by the forces of the marketplace: supply and demand. If stock markets are efficient, then the share price will fully reflect all available information about the company. If a company's shares are not traded on a stock market, or if the market is "thin" (not many active buyers and sellers) or believed to be inefficient, then alternative methods of valuation are required. Once again, the primary form of model for valuing shares comes from the application of present value techniques.

5.6.1   Share price valuation I: The basic model

The monetary benefits to shareholders come in two forms: dividends, and capital gains (or losses). Thus, the value of a share will be the capitalised value of the expected future income stream.

Let P_0 = the current price of a share

P_1 = the expected price of the share at end-period

D_1 = the dividend paid over the next period

The capital gain (loss) over a single time-period will be $(P_1 - P_0)$. The expected rate of return to the shareholder, k_e, is

$$k_e = \frac{P_1 - P_0 + D_1}{P_0}$$

where k_e is (also) known as the market capitalisation rate. From the company's perspective, k_e represents the cost of raising funds via equity; that is, the "cost of equity capital". This equation can be rewritten as:

$$P_0 = \frac{D_1 + P_1}{1 + k_e}$$

which expresses today's share price, P_0, as the discounted value of the expected dividend and the future price at the end of the period.

Example:

> You are considering investment in the shares of Anderton Enterprises plc, which are currently selling at £10. Based on information in the press you fully expect the payment of a dividend of £0.75 per share over the next year. The price of the share is expected to rise to £11.00. Then, your expected rate of return will be

$$k_e = \frac{P_1 - P_0 + D_1}{P_0}$$

$$k_e = \frac{£11 - £10 + £0.75}{£10} = \frac{£1.75}{£10} = 17.5\%$$

Of course, the reliability of this result depends on the accuracy of the predictions for the future dividend and the future price of the share. Using the variant in equation (2) we can determine the price of the share today.

Example:

> According to "experts", the forecasts for Anderton Enterprises plc's dividends and share price next year are £0.75 and £11.00 respectively. If Anderton Enterprises has a cost of equity capital of 13.5% then its current share price should be

$$P_0 = \frac{D_1 + P_1}{1 + k_e}$$

$$P_0 = \frac{£0.75 + £11}{1 + 0.135} = £10.13$$

Suppose that the prevailing market price for Anderton Enterprises' shares was £10.50, which is higher than £10.13. This would imply that the rate of return was below that offered by shares in companies of equivalent risk. Consequently there would a shift in demand from shares in Anderton Enterprises to those offering higher expected return. This would lead to a decline in the price of shares in Anderton Enterprises, and equivalently an increase in its expected return. The prices of other shares of similar risk would rise, and their expected rates of return would diminish until equilibrium was restored with Anderton Enterprises' share price at £10.13. This is yet another example of the process of arbitrage at work. A similar process, albeit in the opposite direction, would ensue if the share price of Anderton Enterprises was less than £10.13.

This last example shows how we can use the share valuation model to determine the current price of a share based on forecasts (expected values) for its dividend and price in the next period (year). We now need to consider extending our analysis further into the future. Extending equation (2) for a second period, we find:

$$P_0 = \frac{D_1 + P_1}{1 + k_e} + \frac{D_2 + P_2}{(1 + k_e)^2}$$

and generalising to T periods:

$$P_0 = \sum_{t=1}^{T} \frac{D_t}{(1+k_e)^t} + \frac{P_t}{(1+k_e)^T}$$

However, this still begs the question as to what determines the value of P_T. The answer is the discounted stream of future payments received from holding the share beyond time T; that is to say, the stream of dividends beyond time T. On the assumption that the firm is a perpetual organisation, we can extend the equation for an infinite time horizon:

$$P_0 = \sum_{t=1}^{\infty} \frac{D_t}{(1 + r)^t}$$

While this equation, the dividend valuation model (DVM), offers a sound method for share price valuation in theory, its usefulness depends on the ability to predict future dividends. Thus, for practical purposes the model is often adjusted to account for a given assumption regarding future dividends. Of these adjustments the Gordon growth model, which we now consider, is probably the most-widely known.

5.6.2   Share price valuation II: The Gordon growth model

One of the simplest assumptions to make about the profile of future dividends is that they will grow at a predetermined rate. Following the work of the economist, Myron Gordon [1959], assume that dividends are expected to grow at a constant rate of $g\%$ per annum; thus

$$D_t = D_{t-1} * (1 + g),$$

alternatively $\qquad\qquad\qquad D_t = D_0*(1 + g)^t$

Substituting into the basic share price valuation model (the DVM) gives

$$P_0 = \sum_{t=1}^{\infty} \frac{D_0 \left(1 + g\right)^t}{\left(1 + k_e\right)^t}$$

$$P_0 = D_0 \sum_{t=1}^{\infty} \frac{\left(1 + g\right)^t}{\left(1 + k_e\right)^t}$$

The summation ($\sum$) term reduces to $\dfrac{\left(1 + g\right)}{(k_e - g)}$, giving:

$$P_0 = \frac{D_0\left(1 + g\right)}{\left(k_e - g\right)}$$

which is more commonly written as:

$$P_0 = \frac{D_1}{k_e - g}$$

This is little more than an example of a constantly growing perpetuity. The *caveat* is that for this formula to make sense the expected growth rate of dividends, $g < k_e$, the cost of equity capital (or, from the investor's viewpoint, the required rate of return on equity). This variant is much easier to use in practical terms than the general share valuation model shown in equation 5. Indeed, even if the assumption of constant dividend growth does not turn out to be correct, this model still offers a good "first approximation" for decision-making purposes.

As with the general share price valuation model, by rearranging the Gordon growth model we can obtain an expression to calculate the cost of equity capital:

$$k_e = \frac{D_1}{P_0} + g$$

where D_1/P_0 is called the "dividend yield". It is not difficult to see that if the expected growth rate of dividends is zero, then the cost of equity capital is equal to the dividend yield.

Example:

> Rosenthal plc have a well-established policy of increasing their dividend each year by 5%. The dividend per share paid this year was £0.20, and the current share price is £1.20. According to the Gordon growth model, the cost of equity capital for Rosenthal plc will be
>
> $$k_e = \frac{£0.20}{£1.20} + 0.05 = 0.2166667 = 21.67\%$$

Gordon's growth model shows the return to shareholders as the sum of the expected return in the form of a dividend over the next time-period plus the growth rate (of dividends). Because next period's dividend is often uncertain, in practice the dividend yield is often computed as D_0/P_0, to which an expected annual growth rate can then be applied.

Of course, the simplest variant of the Gordon growth model is the case where dividends are expected to remain constant at their current level, D, which is the case when the dividend growth rate, g, is zero. In this case the formula reduces to:

$$P_0 = \frac{D}{k_e}$$

or, in cost of capital terms $\qquad k_e = \frac{D}{P_0}$

While the underlying assumption of the Gordon growth model—a constant growth rate of dividends—appears questionable, the model remains widely used in practice and at the very least offers a useful rule-of-thumb measure. Empirically, it is not as questionable as it might seem at first glance. One reason is that major companies often try to maintain relatively stable dividend policies—including a stable growth rate of dividends—especially in view of the large number of institutional investors (such as pension funds) for whom dividends provide a regular income.

Although the Gordon growth model provides an easier method of share price valuation than the more general form, there remain difficulties. It is certain that next year's dividend, D_1, may be uncertain. Nonetheless, it may be possible to make a reliable estimate of D_1 given that this year's dividend will be known with certainty, and that the firm's recent dividend payout policy will be known via trends or via public pronouncements. But there will always remain the difficult task of calculating the growth rate of dividends, g. Perhaps the simplest method is to extrapolate from trends in the recent past. Another alternative is to base dividend growth forecasts on the company's stated dividend policy. Or, one might be guided by the views of professional analysts where they have a track record that suggests their pronouncements to be credible.

5.7   Dividends

The share price valuation model clearly illustrates the importance of dividends to the value of the company as reflected in the price of its shares. Given that the objective of the firm is to maximise its value, and hence the price of its shares, it would be too easy to conclude from the foregoing that a company which has never paid dividends, and therefore seems unlikely to pay dividends in the future, would have zero value. Alternatively, one might be tempted to conclude that a firm should distribute all of its earnings as dividends to maximise its share price. Yet both views would go against the grain of common-sense.

The rationale for these views is based on seeing dividends as the entire focus of the return on equity; which would be the case for a company whose shares are viewed as "income stock". It fails to consider that the shareholder might also make a return in the form of a capital gain through the sale of shares; a company whose shares are viewed as "growth stock". In reality, a profitable company which chooses to retain its earnings does so because it believes it can make a better return on these funds than could the individual shareholders if they were distributed as dividends. If investors in general agree with the firm's view, then there will be a positive demand for the company's shares, and hence a positive share price.

One alternative view is that the value of the firm is the discounted value of its future stream of earnings, regardless of whether or not they are retained or distributed as dividends. This would give the following model:

$$P_0 = \sum_{t=1}^{\infty} \frac{EPS_t}{\left(1 + k_e\right)^t}$$

where EPS_t is the earnings-per-share during time t. Because in the complete fullness of time, the firm's earnings are eventually distributed to the shareholders, it might easily be suggested that equation 10 is identical to equation 5 over the firm's lifespan. This model offers a useful tool for valuing the shares of a company which has a zero dividend payout policy.

The relationship between a company's dividend policy and its earnings (or EPS) can be illustrated by recourse to a series of simple illustrative tales:

1. Consider Cheshunt plc, a firm which decides not to undertake any real investment into the foreseeable future. In the short-term, Cheshunt will be able to pay out all of its earnings as dividends, as it has no need for the funds itself. If shareholders perceive only the short-term, then the price of shares will increase. Alternatively, if shareholders are less myopic then because net investment equals real investment less depreciation, Cheshunt will experience negative net investment, which will increasingly manifest itself through increasing problems with its capital equipment. This will eventually lead to increasing costs of maintenance, which will have a negative impact on profit levels. Lower earnings will ultimately mean lower dividends. Eventually there will be zero dividends when competitor firms who have undertaken investment in new capital find themselves with greater productivity and hence lower costs of production than Cheshunt plc. This would ultimately lead to the demise of the firm. Thus, because the stream of dividends will eventually fall to zero, we would expect the price of the share to drop.

2. Now consider the case of Chigwell plc, which pays no dividends, preferring to retain the earnings to finance the undertaking of internal investment projects. While some of these investments will prove to add value to the firm, there will be others which are less profitable due to the law of diminishing returns. If shareholders

perceive that a firm is using its retained earnings for projects which yield a lower rate of return than the shareholders could achieve themselves if the funds were distributed, they will be tempted to sell off their shareholdings, leading to the ultimate decline in Chigwell plc's share price.

The moral of these tales is straightforward. A firm should retain earnings if it can earn a higher rate of return with them; it should distribute earnings as dividends if shareholders can earn a better rate of return on them.

5.8 Not-quite-equity: Options

Recent dramatic events in the financial world have brought the word "derivatives" into the public domain. The collapse of Barings, and its association with the "rogue trader" Nick Leeson, as well as other spectacularly huge losses due to derivatives' trading, has done little to enhance the credibility of the world of finance in the mind of the ordinary member of the public. Yet derivatives are a large and growing sector of the financial universe.

There are three major types of derivative: **futures**, **options**, and **swaps**. A derivative is a "derived security" because its value is derived from the value of some underlying commodity. The primary *raison d'être* for options is for the hedging of risk. In practice, both equity options (also known as stock options) and currency options exist, as well as more exotic variants such as options on futures and interest rate options. Our concern here is with equity options.

There are two types of equity option: a "call" option and a "put" option. A call option gives the holder the right (but not the obligation) to buy the underlying equity (shares) at a predetermined price *on or before* a given date.[1] A put option gives the holder the right (but not the obligation) to sell the underlying shares at a predetermined price on or before a given date (known as the "expiry date" or "expiration date").

---

[1] This is an example of an "American" option. A "European" option gives the holder the right to buy (sell) at a predetermined price *on* a given date. European options tend to be less common in reality. The terms have no connection to geographical location.

The price paid for the option itself is known as the "option premium", while the amount paid to exercise the option (that is, to buy or sell the underlying shares) is called the "exercise price" or "striking price".

Options can be "exchange-traded" or OTC (over-the-counter). The former are usually standardised, and traded on the specialised derivatives markets. The latter are highly specialised, and lack the standardised qualities to enable them to be traded in a market. Trading in stock options first began in 1973 on the Chicago Board Options Exchange. The London Stock Exchange has had some form of option dealing for well over two centuries, although not continuously, and for some time of quite limited volume. When options are traded in a financial marketplace, the option premium will be determined by the forces of supply and demand. The option premium is usually a small fraction of the price of the underlying share.

There are two sides to every option contract, corresponding to the demand and supply sides of the market. Buying an option is referred to as taking a "long position", whereas taking a "short position" refers to selling (or "writing") an option. An investor who writes an option will receive the option premium for it immediately, but is subject to the (potential) liabilities of meeting the option's requirements later. Theoretically, anyone who can meet the requirements of fulfilling the option contract if (when) it is exercised can issue ("write") an option. In practice, this is very much the domain of full-time professionals.

It is entirely feasible for a company to issue long-term call options on its own shares, known as call "warrants". These are often issued as an attachment to a bond to act as a 'sweetener'. It is also possible for a third party, such as a financial institution, to offer either call or put options on a company's shares. These are known as "covered warrants".

There are four basic positions an investor can take with respect to options:

- A long position in a call option
- A short position in a call option
- A long position in a put option
- A short position in a put option.

Consider the case of a European call option where X = the exercise price and S = the price of the underlying share. There are three possibilities:

If $S > X$ the option is said to be "in the money", and the option is likely to be exercised

If $S < X$ the option is said to be "out of the money" and will not be exercised

If $S = X$ the option is said to be "at the money"

The payoff for the long position in this call will be

$$max.\{S - X, 0\}$$

while for a short position the payoff will be

$$-max.\{S - X, 0\} = min\{X - S, 0\}$$

The value $max.\{S - X, 0\}$ is called the **intrinsic value** of a call option. For a put option the intrinsic value will be $max.\{X - S, 0\}$. Normally, for an American option, the market value of a call option will exceed its intrinsic value:

$$market\ value = intrinsic\ value + time\ value$$

where time value reflects the market's consideration that the price of the option might increase before its expiration date. The time value reflects the "gamble element" inherent in holding the option to expiration rather than exercising it earlier. On the expiration date, there is no time value remaining so the value of the option is its intrinsic value alone.

As with all derivatives, the primary purpose of options is (or, at least, should be) the hedging or management of risk. Consider a (potential) investor in a given company's equity, who believes that the price of these shares will rise over the next few months. This investor can either buy the company's shares or, alternatively, buy call options on the company's shares. The first choice requires the investor to pay out the full price for each of the shares purchased. The second only requires the investor to pay out the option premium (a small fraction) of the share price. If the investor's expectations are unfulfilled because the rise in the share price does not come about, then his losses under the second alternative will be limited to the option premium alone, whereas under the first alternative they could be much larger. Thus, the use of options has allowed the investor to hedge his risk.

Example:

Joey Kinnear is an investor interested in the equity of Mabbutt plc. He expects that the price of these shares will rise from their current market price (S) of 120p. The exercise price of a call option (X) on one share in Mabbutt plc is 100p. The call option thus has an intrinsic value of 120p - 100p = 20p. Joey can either **purchase 50,000 shares** or **go long in call options** to purchase the same number of shares. But, there is always the possibility that the price of shares can go down. By opting for the call options, he can limit his risk to the amount he pays out for the call options, and exercise the options if the share price rises as expected. If Joey decides to buy the shares directly then his exposure to risk is much greater. The following table shows the payoff from either strategy if the share price actually falls:

share price drops to	**buy 50,000 shares** amount of loss	**buy options on 50,000 shares** amount of loss
119p	£500	£500
115p	£2,500	£2,500
110p	£5,000	£5,000
100p	£10,000	£5,000
60p	£25,000	£5,000
20p	£45,000	£5,000
10p	£50,000	£5,000
0	£60,000	£5,000

By adopting the strategy of buying options the maximum loss Joey will sustain is £5,000, whereas there is a potential loss from buying the shares of £60,000. For the option strategy to prove optimal requires the share price to drop by at least the amount of the intrinsic value of the call option.

While this example shows the use of derivatives for hedging risk, they might also be used to generate a "leverage effect", magnifying the gains that might be made buying shares directly. We can illustrate using the price data from the previous example.

Example:

> Suppose that Joey is totally convinced that the share price (*S*) for Mabbutt plc will rise from its current 120p. He has £60,000 available for investment; his choices are either to use the money to **buy Mabbutt plc shares** or to **go long in call options** on Mabbutt plc shares. Under the first option, Joey can purchase 50,000 shares in Mabbutt plc. Alternatively, he might purchase 300,000 Mabbutt call options at a premium of 20p each.
>
> Suppose that Joey's expectations turn out to be fulfilled, and that shares in Mabbutt plc rise to a price of 145p. The intrinsic value of the options will also rise by the same amount. Had Joey bought the shares he will be looking at a capital gain of 25p*50,000 = £12,500. If he had gone long on the call options, however, his gain would be 25p*300,000 = £75,000.

While this seems like an almost magical way in which to make huge gains, the problem with using call options in this speculative manner is that it depends on expectations being fulfilled. Were the share price to go down rather than up as expected, then using options would have cost Joey his entire stake; a very costly prospect. This indicates the importance of the volatility of the underlying share price as a determinant of the market value of a traded option.

There are six major determinants on the price of a (call) option, most of which can be intuitively divined from the foregoing examples:

1. The price of the underlying share (*S*)
2. The exercise price of the option (*X*)
3. The time the option has to go until expiration $(T - t)$
4. The volatility of the price of the underlying share, σ
5. The risk-free rate of interest, *r*
6. Any dividends expected before the option expires (these usually affect the underlying share price)

The classic model for pricing (European) call options is that put forward by Fischer Black and Myron Scholes in 1973. The equation appears much more daunting at first sight than it is. Let *c* be the price of a European call option, then:

$$c = S.N(d_1) - X.e^{-r(T-t)}.N(d_2)$$

where $N(x)$ represents the cumulative probability distribution function for a standardised normal variable (i.e. the probability that the variable will have a value less than x). This is little more than a complex variant on the formula for the intrinsic value of a call option $(S - X)$. The complexities introduced are

- The exercise price (X) is now in present value terms $(X$ is discounted using the risk-free rate as the discount rate). This is because the option is exercised in the future.
- Because both S and X are variables (assumed to be normally distributed), they are expressed in terms of their underlying probability distributions. This helps to account for volatility. Thus:

$$d_1 = \frac{\ln\left(\frac{S}{X}\right) + \left(r + \frac{\sigma^2}{2}\right)(T - t)}{\sigma\sqrt{T - t}}$$

$$d_2 = d_1 - \sigma\sqrt{T - t} = \frac{\ln\left(\frac{S}{X}\right) + \left(r - \frac{\sigma^2}{2}\right)(T - t)}{\sigma\sqrt{T - t}}$$

Many of the more complicated pricing models used by "rocket scientists" employed in the world's major financial districts are variants on this theme.

6. Investment Appraisal: Capital Budgeting

Investment may be best defined as an act of immediate outlay (costs) in the expectation of future benefits. For appraisal of an investment to take place in a scientific manner it must be possible to measure both costs and benefits in quantifiable terms; that is to say, costs and benefits are usually priced in monetary terms. Decision-making is then a process of weighing up the costs of the investment against the benefits it promises, all in present value (PV) terms. If the benefits outweigh the costs then the investment would be a worthwhile undertaking. Larger firms typically will appraise a number of possible investment projects, and then rank them according to specified criteria. Much of what follows in this chapter deals with various techniques for comparing investment costs with (expected) investment benefits.

Financial economists normally distinguish between two major types of investment: **real investment** and **financial investment**. These closely parallel the two kinds of corporate investment: *capital* investments and *spontaneous* investments.

Real investment refers to the purchase of (productive) capital equipment by a firm in the hope of increasing the value of the firm, typically via an increased stream of future profits. While investment is traditionally viewed as the purchase of tangible capital equipment, it is increasingly recognised that real investment in human capital can occur. One example is the case where a student pays out now for education or training in the expectation that it will result in better job opportunities, including higher remuneration levels. The thinking behind employee education and training schemes is similar. From a pure finance perspective, such capital expenditures are characterised by their irreversibility and the long-term nature of the prospective benefits. While this is most often exemplified by purchases of land, buildings, or capital equipment, permanent additions to working capital (e.g. due to an increase in accounts receivable as a result of permanent changes in the firm's credit policy) may also be included. With the relatively recent trend away from industrialisation towards an "information society", investment in intellectual property is increasing in both scope and depth. This trend has created an explosion in research and development (R&D), as well as associated areas such as patents and copyrights.

Financial investment refers to the purchase of a financial asset in the hope of a future income stream via dividends (in the case of equity) or coupons (in the case of bonds) and a possible capital gain (in the case of all financial assets). However, although financial investment may be long-term in nature it is rarely irreversible, and is a very different species to capital investment. For most firms—with the exception of those engaged as financial intermediaries—financial investment is typically short-term, involving the employment of any surplus assets in the purchase of interest-bearing financial instruments. For the financial economist, financial investment is really an act of saving!

In an economic sense, any changes that occur in current assets due to seasonality or cyclical events may be regarded as "spontaneous" investments. This is because they occur not as the direct result of the actions of management but rather due to changing sales levels, for example. Spontaneous investments are typified by short-term benefits, and are more normally classified as changes in working capital.

6.1   Investment Projects

Firms of all sizes undertake investment projects. Nearly every firm that has existed in the past few decades will have considered the possibility of buying a car at some point in its existence. Whether it is a small firm thinking about the purchase of a personal computer, or a multinational looking at the purchase of a large oil tanker, the same basic techniques for investment appraisal will apply. It is useful to classify projects according to certain non-financial criteria:

- **Replacement projects** are those whereby a firm is updating or upgrading its existing capital equipment. This would include the replacement of worn-out or obsolete machinery.

In larger firms the decision to undertake such investments is usually made at the lowest possible level rather than by senior management.

- **Expansion projects** are those whereby existing capacity is increased. This can take the form of simply increasing the amount of capital equipment devoted to a particular task. Alternatively, it can take the form of newer capital equipment being brought in which can do the same work more productively. Such an investment may therefore have elements of both replacement and expansion.
- **Diversification projects** may be considered a special case of expansion, except that the expansion may be into new lines of production. Another form of diversification project is where a company invests to expand geographically.
- **Other projects** include all investments that do not fit easily into the other categories. This category might include investments which are mandated by law, such as those pertaining to environmental controls or health and safety. One might also include mergers and acquisitions here, because very often these incorporate aspects of an "all of the above" nature.

It is rarely the case that a firm will consider undertaking a single investment project in isolation. What is more likely is that a firm will examine an array of potential investments and then undertake those which meet or exceed some form of corporate benchmark. Firms need to recognise the "dependence status" of the various projects they have under review. Some investments will be mutually exclusive. This is when one or more projects offer alternative means of achieving a single goal, requiring only the best alternative to be selected. This is particularly the case with replacement investment, where there may be several machines available to replace the existing machine, for example. Mutually exclusive investments thus require an "accept/reject" decision.

Often a firm will find itself looking at complementary investments. This is the case where the ability to succeed in one investment requires the undertaking of a second, complementary, investment. Where one or more investments are seen as complementary they should be aggregated and appraised *in toto* as a single investment.

6.2   Cashflows

As we shall see, the techniques for appraising proposed capital investment projects are relatively straightforward in concept. The key issue relates to estimating the cashflows to which these techniques of appraisal are applied. Perhaps the most important thing to learn is that it is cashflows and not accounting flows that are relevant. A simple adage is illustrative:

"profits don't pay bills; cash does."

It is entirely feasible for a firm which is profitable on its books to find itself bankrupt because it does not have the cash inflows to meet its immediate expenses. Equally, it also should be noted that there are a number of non-cash items which are part of the equation in calculating profits. Such non-cash items include depreciation and goodwill. For example, if we assume that the only non-cash item in the firm's income statement is depreciation, then by adding back depreciation we can determine a figure for the firm's cashflow from operations (CFO):

CFO = net income + depreciation

However, this "quick and dirty" method is something of an over-simplification. Nonetheless, it works well enough providing depreciation is the only non-cash item on the firm's income (profit and loss) statement, as all other items are associated with cash inflows and outflows.[2]

For greater precision, changes in the company's assets and liabilities must be taken into account. These balance sheet effects on cashflows include the following examples:

---

[2] Basic accounting suggests that
$$net\ income = cash\ inflows - (cash\ expenses + depreciation)$$
Consequently, adding depreciation to both sides yields
$$net\ income + depreciation = cash\ inflows - (cash\ expenses)$$
i.e. $$net\ income + depreciation = cashflows$$

- Any increase in the firm's assets serves to reduce cash: an increase in the firm's accounts receivables means less cash will be collected over the accounting period, or cash may have been paid out to purchase fixed assets.
- Asset decreases such as the sale of fixed assets serve to increase cash.
- An increase in the firm's accounts payable means that the firm is paying out less cash over the accounting period for a given level of supplies. Similarly, an increase in the firm's long-term debt will lead to an inflow of cash.
- If the firm repaid some of its debt during the accounting period this will lead to a decrease in cash.

All of these changes can be summarised in the following table:

	Asset change	Effect on cash
1	increase in assets	reduction
2	decrease in assets	increase
3	increase in liabilities or equity	increase
4	decrease in liabilities or equity	reduction

Based on these simple observations, the cashflow formula may be expanded to the following form:

$$CF = \text{net income} + \text{depreciation} - (\text{net working capital})$$

$$CF = \text{net income} + \text{depreciation} - (\text{change in assets}) + (\text{change in liabilities \& equity})$$

It is this formula that is applied to the accounting statements to derive the statement of cashflows. This statement usually includes three broad groups of cashflows:

- cashflows from operations (CFO)
- cashflows from investing activities
- cashflows from financing activities

For many firms, especially in the industrial and commercial sector, the second group may be limited to cashflows due to interest payments.

Unsurprisingly, the ability to determine a projected figure for the firm's net income begins with a robust projection for future sales. The cashflows which are pertinent for the purposes of capital budgeting are those which have yet to occur—expected cashflows—and therefore must be estimated. The validity of any investment decision depends crucially on the robustness of these future cashflow estimates. Cashflows which occur before the decision date are referred to as "sunk costs", and are not considered as relevant to the capital budgeting decision. Those cashflows which are important are the incremental cashflows: the difference in cashflows to the firm with the project and without the project. This truly measures the cashflows to the firm that the new project *per se* will generate. If a firm was contemplating a new product line that might compete with any of its existing products, then the possible loss of revenue from the existing products (known as "cannibalisation") must be included as part of the cashflow estimation. Equally, there may be some economies of scale which arise as the result of the new investment. By considering incremental cashflows, these issues are all properly addressed.

Additionally, cashflows must be estimated on a post-tax basis. From the firm's perspective, taxes are a cost of doing business like any other and must be treated accordingly. In countries such as the United Kingdom and the United States, the tax law is such that depreciation (and other non-cash items) will affect the firm's earnings before taxation, and consequently the firm's tax bill. Therefore, because depreciation can have an indirect impact on the firm's cashflows, the latter must include any depreciation tax benefits. This same is true of any other non-cash items that will indirectly impact the firm's cashflows. The importance of accurate, well-researched cashflow estimates for the capital budgeting decision cannot be overstated, both from the viewpoint of the firm's well-being and that of the investment analyst. While no amount of accurate information and research can guarantee the future outcome of an investment project, poor information and research leads to poor decision-making.

6.3   Investment Appraisal: Basic (Non-DCF) Methods

Human nature includes a general reluctance to embrace change: "if it ain't broke, don't fix it". Moreover, there is often a reluctance even to recognise when change is required. This is certainly the case with the practise of investment appraisal. Historically, there was once a time when the time value of money was not recognised, and so techniques of investment appraisal relied on non-DCF methods. Michael Bromwich [1976] was moved to write

> The businessman's attitude may be also affected by the dominance of the firm's information system by accountants, who in general have not been trained in the techniques [of discounted cashflows] ..., and whose professional attitudes may possibly militate against their acceptance.

Times have now changed, and discounted cashflows are part and parcel of the curriculum of the various professional accounting bodies' examinations. And yet, there are still some firms who cling on to older methods, even when they have become superseded by more scientifically valid techniques.

6.3.1   The payback period
Under this criterion, those investments which recover the principal (i.e., the initial capital outlay) in the shortest period of time are selected. There are two simple methods of calculating the payback period, depending on the nature of the cashflows:

a)   if the cashflows are regular (even), then

$$\text{payback period} = \frac{\text{net investment}}{\text{annual net cash flows}}$$

b)   if the cashflows are irregular (uneven), then it is necessary to find the point in time when the cumulative cash inflows just equal the (original) net investment:

$$\text{payback period} = t + \frac{c}{(c - d)}$$

where t = the last full year in which the cumulative net cash inflows are less than net investment;
c = cumulative cash flow at time t; and
d = cumulative cash flow at time $t + 1$.

Example:

The Mullery Corporation is considering two investment projects with the following cashflows for the next six years:

year	Project A net cash flow after tax	Project A cumulative cash flow	Project B net cash flow after tax	Project B cumulative cash flow
0	−50,000	−50,000	−50,000	−50,000
1	12,500	−37,500	5,000	−45,000
2	12,500	−25,000	10,000	−35,000
3	12,500	−12,500	15,000	−20,000
4	12,500	0	15,000	−5,000
5	12,500	12,500	25,000	20,000
6	12,500	25,000	30,000	50,000

Project A has regular cashflows of £12,500 each year. Therefore it has a payback period of (50,000/12,500) = 4 years.

Project B has uneven cashflows, increasing from £5,000 to £30,000. Its payback period is therefore 4 − {(-5,000)/(20,000+5,000)} = 4.2 years

Because both projects have the same initial outlay, Project A is preferred to Project B as it recoups the initial outlay quicker. Project A is therefore considered less risky. The payback period would typically be compared with a benchmark used by the company. For example, a company's Board of Directors might decide that projects which are likely to take longer than five years to pay back the initial investment will be unacceptable to their shareholders, and therefore are too risky.

The payback period criterion is often criticised as a method of investment appraisal because it ignores any cashflows which occur after the payback date. Also, it fails to take into account the time value of money. One possible workround is to calculate the payback period on a present value basis. Nonetheless, in practice it is often used as a risk-filtering device in combination with a discounted cashflow (DCF) technique.

6.3.2   The finite horizon criterion

This involves the setting of a terminal date beyond which any prospective cashflows are neglected. The major rationale behind this approach is that not only is the future uncertain, but the greater is that uncertainty the further into the future one attempts to delve. Both this and the payback period criterion depend heavily on an arbitrarily chosen period of time and are, therefore, likely to lead to some rather peculiar and often indefensible conclusions.

6.3.3   Accounting Rate of Return

The Accounting Rate of Return (ARR) is based on accounting (accrual) concepts and not cashflows. At its broadest, it is defined as net income divided by the book value of equity. Because ARR is based on figures in published financial statements it is considered by some to be a particularly practical measure, especially by users of financial statements such as practicing accountants, information intermediaries, loan officers and government policy advisers. When applied to the capital budgeting decision it is defined as:

$$\text{Accounting Rate of Return, ARR} = \frac{\text{profit}}{\text{capital outlay}}$$

where profit is typically calculated as an annual average, usually net of accounting depreciation, and capital outlay can be the initial capital sum, or an annual average with or without the working capital. Note that while projects with higher values of ARR are preferable, companies will usually have in mind a target rate which they will use as a benchmark, only undertaking projects with an ARR above the benchmark.

Note that the ARR makes no use of the time value of money, a major criticism of the approach. And yet (for example) in a 1980 US survey, *Impediments to Capital Formation*, Blume, Friend and Westerfield found 42 per cent of respondents making use of ARR, albeit often in conjunction with another (usually DCF) method.

6.3.4   Profitability index

The profitability index (PI) is a cost-benefit ratio involving the time value of money. It is defined as the ratio of the present value of estimated future cash flows divided by the initial investment; i.e.

$$\text{profitability index, PI} = \frac{\text{PV(future cash flows)}}{-I_0}$$

For an investment to be profitable, and therefore worthy of the firm's consideration, it must have a PI greater than one. Many analysts regard the PI as somewhat simplistic. It is also the case that the PI can typically deduce rankings that are inconsistent with the present value criterion, which we consider below. However, because the PI indicates which projects will maximise the rate of return for each pound spent on the initial investment, it offers a useful decision-making indicator when a firm finds itself in a position of "capital rationing" (best defined as a shortage of funds that forces a company to choose between worthwhile projects). Note that capital rationing can occur due to the company setting a cap on its capital expenditures, as well as due to external constraints (see Section 6.4.3).

6.4   Investment Appraisal: Discounted CashFlow (DCF) techniques

6.4.1   Net Present Value

Net Present Value (NPV) is the discounted value of the sum of net cashflows generated by an investment project less any initial outlay on the project. Thus:

$$NPV = \sum_{t=1}^{T} \frac{CF_t}{(1 + k)^t} - I_0$$

where CF_t = net cashflows during period t; k = the appropriate discount rate (or cost of capital); I_0 = initial outlay. The Net Present Value rule is:

NPV > 0	the project is acceptable
NPV < 0	reject the project

Projects with a positive NPV are acceptable and will increase the value of the firm by the value of the NPV. However, simply because a project is considered acceptable does not mean that the firm should undertake it. The investment should be compared with other possible investment projects in terms of their Net Present Values. A ranking or league-table of investments based on their NPVs may then be constructed. Projects with higher NPVs should be undertaken first.

Example:

Blanchflower Creative plc is considering the outlay of £50,000 for equipment that will yield a series of increasing cashflows over a six-year time-horizon, after which the equipment will have no salvage value. If the discount rate is 14% the following will prevail:

year	CF	PV factor @ 14%	PV (CF)
1	5,000	0.877	4,385
2	10,000	0.769	7,690
3	15,000	0.675	10,125
4	15,000	0.592	8,880
5	25,000	0.519	12,975
6	30,000	0.456	13,680
			57,735
		less I	50,000
		NPV	7,735

The NPV of this project is positive indicating that if the project were undertaken **the value of the firm would be increased by £7,735**. Thus, the firm should regard this project as acceptable. If this is the only project under consideration, then the firm should undertake it.

What if Blanchflower Creative plc was considering the cashflows in the previous example but was subject to a higher discount rate, say 20 per cent? This would result in the following:

year	CF	PV factor @ 20%	PV (CF)
1	5,000	0.8333	4,167
2	10,000	0.6944	6,994
3	15,000	0.5787	8,681
4	15,000	0.4823	7,234
5	25,000	0.4019	10,047
6	30,000	0.3349	10,047
			47,119
		less I	50,000
		NPV	(2,881)

Now, the NPV of this project is negative indicating that if the project were undertaken *the value of the firm would be decreased by £2,881.* Thus, the firm should regard this project as unacceptable. However, it is also important to note that when the discount rate is increased, the corresponding NPV diminishes. This illustrates the inverse relationship between a project's NPV and the discount rate applied. We can show this inverse relationship more fully in graphical format:

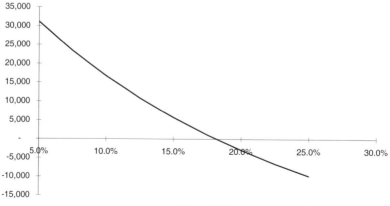

Discount Rate

In the preceding examples the firm is considering the undertaking of an independent project: a single investment project in isolation. If the NPV is greater than zero the project is considered to be worthwhile (in that it will add value to the firm). However, given that most firms usually have a limited amount of funding available for investment, it is more likely that the firm will examine an array of possible independent investments, and then rank them according to the resulting NPV. The firm will then undertake the project with the highest NPV; if further funding is available it will then take on the project with the second-highest NPV; and so on until all funding for investment projects is exhausted (see Section 6.4.3) or the remaining projects fail to meet or exceed the firm's benchmark NPV.

Nonetheless, firms need to recognise that some investments under review will be mutually exclusive. That is to say, that one or more investment projects offer alternative means of achieving a single goal; therefore only the best alternative needs to be selected. A prime example of mutually exclusive projects might be a firm considering replacing its current equipment with newer equipment. In such a case, although one might easily compare NPVs, it is sometimes simpler to find the NPV for the differential cashflows between the two alternatives. We consider the implications of mutually exclusive investments further in Section 6.5.

It is also worth noting that any firm is essentially a portfolio of the investment projects it undertakes. On that basis, and because NPVs are additive, we could value a firm as the sum of the NPVs of its investment projects.

The choice of an appropriate discount rate is invariably problematic. The discount rate should reflect how much it will cost the firm to obtain the funding necessary to undertake its investment project(s). Firms usually employ the **cost of capital** (a measure of the average cost of funds, covered fully in Chapter Eight), which typically reflects the market's determination of the risk involved in undertaking the project. But even this has its problems, as there may be no clear way to estimate it. The cost of capital is historically-based and may not reflect the future within which the project is located. Many companies nowadays specify a "hurdle rate" cost of capital, which incorporates the firm's own estimation of the risk involved, although such firms are extraordinarily reluctant to reveal how it has been determined, or even what value it takes! Down the years most studies of British industry's cost of capital have found it to be much higher than market estimates would suggest. Stockbrokers argue that it is in high single digits, and yet companies often prefer a hurdle rate somewhere in the twenty per cent range. Given these difficulties, there should be little problem understanding why another DCF (discounted cashflow) technique for appraising capital investment projects is required.

6.4.2   Internal Rate of Return (IRR)

The Internal Rate of Return (ρ) is that discount rate which gives an investment project a Net Present Value (NPV) of zero. Thus:

$$NPV = 0 = \sum_{t=1}^{T} \frac{CF_t}{(1 + \rho)^t} - I_0$$

Alternatively
$$\sum_{t=1}^{T} \frac{CF_t}{(1 + \rho)^t} = I_0$$

The Internal Rate of Return may be found by trial-and-error, which is old-fashioned but effective, or with the aid of a financial calculator. More common nowadays is the use of spreadsheet functions, such as those found in (e.g.) Microsoft® Excel™. In each case, a guess is made for a starting value for the IRR; the NPV for this guess is then calculated.

- If the NPV turns out to be positive, then the next guess for the IRR must be higher (due to the negative relationship between the discount rate and NPV).
- If the NPV turns out to be negative, then a lower value guess of IRR must be chosen.

This process of plugging in guesses of the value of IRR continues until IRR is found such that the NPV is equal to zero.[3] Once the IRR has been determined it can then be measured against a reference rate, usually the cost of acquiring funds (r):

$$\rho > r \qquad \text{the project is acceptable}$$

$$\rho < r \qquad \text{reject the project}$$

Example 1: Trial-and-Error

William Nicholson is planning to start his own business. He estimates start-up costs of £70,000 and expects to net the following income in the first five years: £12,000, £15,000, £18,000, £21,000, and £26,000. Internal rate of return, ρ, is that discount rate which gives an investment project a NPV of zero. Thus:

$$\frac{£12,000}{\left(1 + \rho\right)^1} + \frac{£15,000}{\left(1 + \rho\right)^2} + \frac{£18,000}{\left(1 + \rho\right)^3} + \frac{£21,000}{\left(1 + \rho\right)^4} + \frac{£26,000}{\left(1 + \rho\right)^5} = £70,000$$

Substituting $\rho = 0.1 = 10\%$ into the above equation gives:

$$\frac{£12,000}{\left(1.1\right)^1} + \frac{£15,000}{\left(1.1\right)^2} + \frac{£18,000}{\left(1.1\right)^3} + \frac{£21,000}{\left(1.1\right)^4} + \frac{£26,000}{\left(1.1\right)^5} = £70,000$$

Calculating the present value interest factors (the denominators) gives:

---

[3] In the case of a computerised spreadsheet this iterative process is performed by the software. Nonetheless, even state-of-the-art software requires a starting guess, which is set by default to 10 per cent. Thus, in Microsoft® Excel™ the formula appears:

= IRR(values, guess)

According to the manual:

"**Values** is an array or a reference to cells that contain numbers for which you want to calculate the internal rate of return.

Guess is a number that you guess is close to the result of IRR.

Microsoft Excel uses an iterative technique for calculating IRR. Starting with guess, IRR cycles through the calculation until the result is accurate within 0.00001 percent."

$$\frac{£12,000}{(1.1)^1} + \frac{£15,000}{(1.21)^2} + \frac{£18,000}{(1.331)^3} + \frac{£21,000}{(1.4641)^4} + \frac{£26,000}{(1.61051)^5} = £70,000$$

which gives NPV = £10,909.09 + £12,396.69 + £13,523.67 + £14,343.28 + £16,143.95 − £70,000

Thus **NPV = −£2,683.31**

Clearly this value of ρ is too high, as it gives an NPV less than zero. The true IRR must be somewhat lower than 10 per cent. Try ρ = 8%:

$$\frac{£12,000}{(1.08)^1} + \frac{£15,000}{(1.08)^2} + \frac{£18,000}{(1.08)^3} + \frac{£21,000}{(1.08)^4} + \frac{£26,000}{(1.08)^5} = £70,000$$

which gives NPV = £11,111.11 + £12,860.08 + £14,288.98 + £15,435.63 + £17,695.16

Thus **NPV = £1,390.96**

This value of ρ is too high, as it gives an NPV greater than zero. The true IRR must be lower than 10 per cent but higher than 8 per cent. Successive approximations for the value of ρ indicate that it is 8.66%

Although trial-and-error offers a foolproof method for accurately determining the Internal Rate of Return (IRR) of an investment project, it is both tedious and time-consuming. One way of circumventing the need for successive iterations is to find two discount rates that correspond to a positive and negative NPV respectively, and then by interpolation calculate an approximate value for IRR. In the "William Nicholson" example we found the following:

discount rate	NPV
ρ_1 = 8 %	NPV_1 = £1,390.96
ρ_2 = 10 %	NPV_2 = −£2,683.31

It is quite apparent from this that the Internal Rate of Return (IRR) lies somewhere between 8% and 10%. This can be clearly seen on a graph of Net Present Value (NPV) against the discount rate:

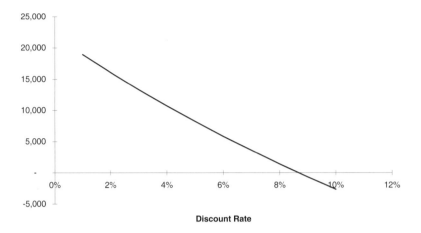

Discount Rate

If we assume that the slope of the graph is, or approximates, a straight line, then we can use the following formula to calculate an approximate value for the Internal Rate of Return:

$$\rho* = \frac{\rho_2 NPV_1 - \rho_1 NPV_2}{NPV_1 - NPV_2}$$

Applying this to the "William Nicholson" example gives:

$$\rho* = \frac{0.1*(1,390.96) - 0.08*(-2,683.31)}{1,390.96 - (-2,683.31)} = 0.0868$$

i.e. an Internal Rate of Return of 8.68%. A quick glance at the graph above confirms this result. However, it should be emphasised that this is an approximation—the actual result calculated above is 8.66%—based on the assumption of a linear relationship between NPV and the discount rate. Although in this example the difference between the actual result and the approximation is quite small, in many cases the difference may prove to be substantial, and any approximated IRR should be used with the appropriate caution.

While calculation of the Internal Rate of Return "by hand" can be quite tedious, the use of modern computer spreadsheets (as previously noted) makes light work of such calculations, increasing the attractiveness of this method of capital budgeting appraisal. Nonetheless, it is worth noting that each software application has its own idiosyncrasies; for example, using Microsoft® Excel™, the Net Present Value function works on the assumption that the first cashflow occurs in year 1 (rather than year 0); this is *not* the case for Excel's IRR function.

Finally, it is worth noting that there are some variants on the IRR method, especially "dual-rate" schemes, where one rate is used for discounting up to payback, and a different rate subsequently. This involves effectively dividing the project into two parts: first, when the project is a net borrower (and thus riskier); and second, when the project has a cash surplus (and thus lower risk).

Having calculated the IRR, a decision on whether or not the project is feasible needs to be made. As we saw on page 119, this involves comparison with the cost of acquiring funds (the cost of capital). In Section 6.5 we compare the IRR and NPV methods of investment appraisal.

6.4.3   Capital rationing

Under the idealistic circumstances posited by economic theory, a firm would undertake all potential projects which satisfied its capital budgeting criterion. Thus, a firm using the Net Present Value method for appraising its investments would undertake each and every project with a positive Net Present Value; a firm using the Internal Rate of Return method would undertake each and every project with an IRR greater than the firm's hurdle rate cost of capital. However, the real world has a tendency to differ from that of economic theory, and firms frequently find themselves restricted in the amounts of financing they are willing (or perhaps able) to utilise for capital expenditures. When this is the case "capital rationing" is said to occur.

It should be noted that in cases of capital rationing the firm is failing to undertake projects which would help it pursue the objective of maximising its value. Thus, capital rationing implies that value maximisation is not an objective of the firm *per se*; rather the firm's objective is value maximisation subject to the firm's capital ceiling, i.e. constrained value maximisation.

Financial managers facing capital rationing should, therefore, pursue the objective of maximising the sum of the Net Present Values of those projects selected. This will typically take place (as we have seen) by ranking potential investment projects in terms of their NPV, and undertaking those at the top (e.g. with the highest NPV) then moving down the list to those projects with lower NPVs until the capital ceiling is reached.

6.5   Comparison of NPV with IRR

Given that both the Net Present Value (NPV) and Internal Rate of Return (IRR) techniques are discounted cashflow (DCF) techniques of investment appraisal, the question arises as to which method—if any—offers superior recommendations.

Because firms rely on these DCF techniques to make decisions on capital expenditure, it is important that the results have credibility. For example, expected values such as the projected cash flows need to be wholly believable by the decision-makers. It should always be possible to justify the projected data with sound, rational argument. Unlike other aspects of a firm's decision-making, the capital expenditure decision is one involving an inflexible long-term commitment. Most capital equipment is highly specialised in its usage, and for most equipment there is rarely a well-ordered secondary market. Thus, a capital expenditure decision which proves to be ill-fated is not one that can be turned around in short order.

6.5.1   Number of solutions
One of the advantages offered by NPV is that it will always lead to a unique conclusion, whereas IRR may yield multiple solutions. By way of example consider the following three-period cashflow profile:

$$I_0, \quad CF_1, \quad CF_2$$

where I_0 represents the initial outlay to finance the investment, and CF_t are the net cashflows in year t. To find the IRR we must solve the equation

$$\frac{CF_1}{(1+\rho)} + \frac{CF_2}{(1+\rho)^2} - I_0 = 0$$

By the process of cross-multiplication this can be rewritten as

$$-I_0(1+\rho)^2 + CF_1(1+\rho) + CF_2 = 0$$

which is a quadratic equation in $(1+\rho)$. Quadratic equations are well-known to have two possible solutions (known as "roots"), although it might turn out that the two roots are identical.

If the cashflows were for a time-horizon of more than three time-periods, then IRR calculations would result in a polynomial equation: a four-period cashflow profile would result in a cubic equation, yielding three roots; a five-year cashflow profile would result in a quartic equation, which has four roots; and so on:

- The formula for IRR will always yield a polynomial of degree n, which has n-1 roots, where n refers to the number of time-periods.

Under these circumstances the question as to which root is economically meaningful for the purposes of capital budgeting is crucial.[4] Fortunately, in practise most roots turn out to be negative or imaginary, implying that they can be ignored providing that at least one root turns out to be positive.

- Descartes' "change of sign rule" suggests that there will be as many positive roots as there are changes in sign for the cashflow.

Thus, if the net cashflow is always positive after the initial outlay then there will be a single positive root for $(1+\rho)$, implying a unique solution for ρ.

---

[4] The existence of multiple roots was first noted by J. H. Lorie and L. J. Savage (1955)

It is worth noting that in the case where the appraisal is of a single independent investment project, and thus the only decision is either to accept or reject the project, NPV and IRR calculations yield identical recommendations: whenever NPV is positive, the IRR (ρ) will exceed the cost of capital, and *vice versa*. This is a mathematical truism when the NPV of a project is a smoothly declining function of the discount rate.

However, when the firm is ranking a range of possible investment projects or considering mutually exclusive investments, it is entirely feasible that the Net Present Value and Internal Rate of Return appraisals will offer *different* recommendations. As we shall see, because IRR might proffer the wrong recommendation most analysts tend to prefer the NPV method:

Example:

Klinsmann*Geselleschaft* is considering two mutually exclusive investment projects with the following cashflow profiles:

	0	1	2	3
Project X	-£216,500	£102,838	£102,838	£102,838
Project Y	-£108,250	£55,424	£55,424	£55,424

A comparison of the results from using the two DCF methods for investment appraisal is intriguing:

	NPV @ 10%	IRR
Project X	£39,242.89	20%
Project Y	£29,581.28	25%

According to the Net Present Value method, Project X should be chosen as it adds £39,242.89 to the value of the firm (more than Project Y's £29,581.28). However, this contrasts with the recommendation of the Internal Rate of Return method, which has Project Y with the superior rate of return: 25% as compared to X's 20%.

Because the NPV method relates directly to the firm's objective (to maximise its value), its recommendation can be seen as intuitively superior. However, when considering why the NPV and IRR methods offer different recommendations we can establish more clearly the superiority of NPV, as well as methods for adapting the IRR method so that it also offers correct recommendations.

6.5.2 Scale and duration

In the previous example there was a difference in the scale of the two projects being considered by Klinsmann*Geselleschaft*: Project X required an initial outlay of £216,500 while Project Y only required an initial outlay of £108,250. Given this difference in scale, we may consider Project X to be the "economic equivalent" of Project Y plus an additional project (Project F) which consists of the differential cashflow between X and Y, thus:

	0	1	2	3
Project X	−£216,500	£102,838	£102,838	£102,838
Project Y	−£108,250	£55,424	£55,424	£55,424
Project F	−£108,250	£47,414	£47,414	£47,414

Project F has an NPV of £9,661.60 and an IRR of 15%. Thus we may consider Project X to be the same as undertaking both Project Y and Project F: it will give a combined NPV of £29,581.28 + £9,661.60 = £39,242.89 (the same as the NPV of Project X). However, Project F yields an IRR of 15%; thus *Project X's IRR is a weighted average of the IRRs from Project F and Project Y*. From this we may deduce that IRR offers us an "average" measure of the investment, with no regard to its size, whereas NPV offers an absolute measure which does take the size of the investment into account.

A similar perspective may be taken when we consider two projects of unequal duration. A simple comparison between their respective NPVs would not be comparing like with like, so more information is required for a rational decision. Consider the following:

Example:

> The town of Harmer is on a small island and can only be reached by a
> road-bridge, which only has about a year of useful life remaining. The
> town council is considering different alternative replacements, of which
> there are two front-runners: Bridge 1 involves a wooden bridge with a
> predicted lifespan of five years, Bridge 2 involves a steel bridge with a
> predicted lifespan of nine years. Both bridges would offer the same level
> of service during each year of its existence.

Obviously, these two alternatives cannot be directly compared using
NPV (or any other technique): firstly, the wooden bridge would require
much more frequent maintenance, and secondly it would also require
more frequent replacement. Ideally, what would make for a proper
comparison would be a succession of bridges of both steel and wood of
the same duration. Diagrammatically this would appear as follows:

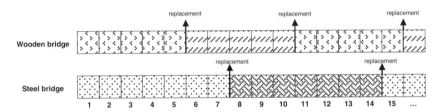

As the diagram indicates, it would take thirty five years before we reach
the first occasion on which the duration of a succession of both bridges
would be equal. In theory we might conduct a NPV analysis comparing a
succession of seven wooden bridges with five steel bridges. In practice
this is obviously not practicable, because (for example) the expected cash
flows—including the price of bridges in the future—are completely
uncertain. Nonetheless, this theoretically sound technique can be
extended into a more practical alternative.

Rather than consider some uncertain set of cash flows for each of the
two possible alternatives, a better method would be to compare the value
added by each on a *per annum* basis; a form of seeking "annual
equivalence" by which the two projects can then be compared in
perpetuity. This is done using the following steps:

- Calculate the NPV for each of the original projects over the course of their original lifespan (call it t years), using the appropriate cost of capital, k. Refer to these calculations as NPV_1. In the bridge example above, there will be an NPV_1 for the wooden bridge (NPV_{1w}) and an NPV1 for the steel bridge (NPV_{1s}).
- Divide the calculated value NPV_1 by the present value interest factor for an annuity of t years at the same cost of capital, k (see Section 3.5.2, page 62). This has the effect of converting the original cash flows into an **equivalent annual annuity**, a, which will offer the same NPV as the original set of cash flows using the same values of t and k. This step is performed for both alternatives, so that there will be an a_w and a_s for the wooden and steel bridges respectively.
- The final step is to divide the equivalent annual annuity, a, by the appropriate discount rate, k. This calculation will provide NPV_∞, that is the Net Present Value of the equivalent annual annuity *in perpetuity*. Again, this is performed for each of the alternative project proposals, which can then be compared for a decision to be made.

The three steps outlined above can be summarised using the following equation:

$$NPV_\infty = \frac{\dfrac{NPV_t}{PVIFA_{t,k}}}{k} = \frac{a}{k}$$

6.6   In Summary: Some General Guidelines for Capital Budgeting

- Always use cash flows, not accounting flows.
- Consider incremental cash flows when they occur. The financial impact of a project is measured by the incremental cash flows: i.e. new cash flows less old cash flows
- Use after-tax cash flows, and therefore include tax effects.

- Accountants typically separate current expenses from capital expenses; don't!
- Use allocated costs with considerable care as these are often based on subjective judgements.
- Never include sunk costs (i.e. costs which have already been met); "let bygones be bygones".
- Separate the investment decision from the financing decision: do not include financing costs, at least in the first instance.
- Ensure the discount rate chosen reflects the project risk. Consider:
    - Should revenues and costs be discounted at the same rate?
    - Should the same discount rate be applied for each time period?
- Treat inflation consistently (see Section 6.7 below).
- Examine the sensitivity of the capital budgeting decision to key factors (see Section 6.8 below).
- Ensure cash inflows in any time-period are adequate to meet cash outflows.
- NPV measures how much the firm is expected to increase in value in *absolute* terms; IRR is a *relative* measure, but has nothing to say about size.
- Some problems with IRR (ρ):
    - multiple solutions may occur if there are a number of changes of sign in the cashflows;
    - project scale is ignored;
    - IRR assumes all cashflows are reinvested at IRR (ρ rate);
    - IRR is not suitable in a situation of capital rationing because it does not consider project scale.

6.7   Real and nominal values

Economists like to make a distinction between **real** values and **nominal** values. Traditionally, most prices are denominated in nominal values, which means that goods are priced in terms of the unit of currency contemporaneously. However, in the modern economic environment we tend to experience ongoing inflation. This means that the value of the currency itself is depreciating, and may therefore give a false sense of value to goods priced in that currency; this is known as "money illusion".[5] One economic variable which is immediately impacted by inflation is the rate of interest. All interest rates typically incorporate an "inflation premium" to offset the declining purchasing power of money occasioned by inflation. This will further impact the firm's overall cost of capital, and thus its capital budgeting decision.

It is crucial, therefore, that capital budgeting values are denominated either entirely in real terms or entirely in nominal terms. Any inconsistency is likely to lead to a downward bias in the investment decision, as the following illustrates:

Example:

Mackay Steelworks is planning investment in a new plant which would yield £250,000 *per annum* over five years. The cost of the plant is £1,000,000, and the applicable cost of capital (the discount rate) is 7 per cent. Assuming no inflation, the Net Present Value of this project is

$$\text{NPV} = \sum_{t=1}^{T} \frac{CF_t}{(1 + \rho)^t} - I$$

$$\text{NPV} = \sum_{t=1}^{5} \frac{£250,000}{(1 + 0.7)^t} - £1,000,000 = £25,049$$

In this example, the nominal cost of capital (7%) is also the real cost of capital. Now consider how this would be affected by an inflation rate

---

[5] Most economists would argue that "money illusion" is irrational. However, in reality it may not always be easy to distinguish a rise in the price of a given commodity from a (sustained) rise in the general price level. Only the latter is inflation.

of 3 per cent, which is expected to prevail over the five-year life of the project. Based on the **Fisher equation**, the following relationship exists:[6]

$$(1 + k)(1 + \pi) = (1 + k^*)$$

where k^* is the cost of capital in nominal terms, k is the cost of capital in real terms, and π is the expected rate of inflation. From this we find that the nominal cost of capital is

$$k^* = [(1 + k)(1 + \pi)] - 1$$

which comes out to be 10.21%. Obviously, if we were to recalculate the Net Present Value using this higher (nominal) cost of capital we would obtain a lower NPV:

$$NPV = \sum_{t=1}^{5} \frac{£250,000}{(1 + 0.1021)^t} - £1,000,000 = -£57,366$$

Thus, a moderate inflation level of 3% leads to a project being rejected which was acceptable when there was zero inflation.

However, this is to ignore the fact that the cashflows are also likely to be affected by inflation. On the assumption that the cashflows grow in line with the rate of inflation, the capital budgeting problem becomes:

$$NPV = \sum_{t=1}^{5} \frac{£250,0000(1 + 0.03)^t}{(1 + 0.07)^t(1 + 0.03)^t} - £1,000,000$$

$$= \sum_{t=1}^{5} \frac{£250,000}{(1 + 0.07)^t} - £1,000,000$$

Thus, with inflation included in both numerator and denominator we arrive back at our original calculation! Consistency has been assured.

---

[6] Based on the work of the American economist Irving Fisher in his *Theory of Interest* (1930), the Fisher equation is usually approximated as

$$...i_{nominal} = i_{real} + expected\ inflation$$

6.8   Sensitivity and Scenario Analysis

When using a discounted cashflow (DCF) technique to consider the undertaking of a capital investment project, the discount rate chosen should normally be one which incorporates the right degree of risk for the project under consideration. It is customary for riskier projects to have their cashflows discounted by a higher cost of capital. For larger firms it may be possible (and is desirable) to use a market-determined cost of capital in their calculations. However, smaller firms and those with a more conservative outlook generally may prefer to make use of variations on DCF techniques for dealing with risk. This may be because they do not have the expertise to quantify the risk, or because the cost of quantifying risk in a scientific manner far outweighs the possible benefits.

It is also true that the credibility of any DCF calculation depends to a very large degree on the quality of the cashflow forecasts being utilised. Accurate cashflow forecasts will lead to better decision-making. In order to compensate for the uncertainty of the future, variations on DCF techniques may be applied to give a clearer picture of the impact of the uncertainty. These variations are known respectively as sensitivity and scenario analysis.

6.8.1   Sensitivity analysis

Sensitivity analysis takes place when the capital budgeting decision is recalculated to see how it reacts to changes in a single key variable. For example, if a firm is heavily reliant on financing its project through floating-rate debt, it may wish to consider how sensitive the accept/reject decision will be to changes in the rate of interest. The firm may therefore calculate (e.g.) the project's NPV based on a series of different rates of interest. If the NPV remains relatively stable regardless of the rate of interest, the project may be considered to be insensitive ("robust") to changes in that variable.

The key issue is for the firm to identify which variables it considers to be particularly crucial to the success of the project and examine how changes in them (individually) will impact the capital budgeting decision. While this will tend to vary according to the nature of the individual characteristics of the investment project being undertaken, there are some variables to which the investment decision is more likely to be sensitive: these would typically include the cost of capital and the sales forecast. Given that the cost of capital is typically given in the financial marketplace, its variation for sensitivity analysis can be considered unrealistic. However, the sales forecast is often a crucial determinant of other cashflows used in the appraisal.

While it may be considered beneficial to examine the sensitivity of the accept/reject decision in terms of a range of values for the key variable, it can also be quite costly in terms of both time and convenience. Consequently, many firms opt for a range of three values: one which represents the "best estimate" for the variable, a second which represents an optimistic assumption, and a third which represents a pessimistic assumption. There is no particular rule for use of sensitivity analysis; rather the firm must make its judgement on the basis of the numbers which ensue. Nonetheless, because the use of sensitivity analysis offers additional information for making the final decision on a particular investment, it should enable the financial manager to make a more informed judgement.

6.8.2   Scenario analysis

Scenario analysis is not unlike sensitivity analysis. The key difference is that whereas sensitivity analysis considers the robustness of the investment decision to changes in a *single* key variable, scenario analysis considers the robustness of the investment decision to changes in a *range* of key variables. Once again, the calculations typically are minimised to a consideration of a baseline scenario, an optimistic scenario, and a pessimistic scenario. Thus, for example, a pessimistic scenario may assume a worst-estimate case for the sales forecast, and the highest possible value for the cost of capital.

One way in which scenario analysis is sometimes used is to determine the breakeven position for a project. As with sensitivity analysis, there is no particular rule for use of scenario analysis. The firm must make its judgement on the basis of the numbers which ensue.

6.9   Newer Approaches to Capital Budgeting

In recent years a newer theoretical approach to capital budgeting has been put forward by a number of well-known financial economists. This view, perhaps most clearly expounded by Avinash Dixit and Robert Pindyck (1994), is based on the application of option-pricing theory to capital budgeting. They argue that their view is superior to "traditional" methods of capital budgeting (such as NPV) because, unlike traditional methods, it offers an explanation of observable phenomena such as why firms often employ a hurdle rate cost of capital which is substantially higher than that observed in the market.

According to Dixit and Pindyck, investment decisions share three key characteristics to varying degrees:

- they are irreversible (partially or completely)
- there is uncertainty over the future rewards
- there is some leeway over the timing

Additionally:

> a firm with an opportunity to invest is holding an "option" analogous to a financial call option—it has the right but not the obligation to buy an asset at some future time of its choosing. When a firm makes an irreversible investment expenditure, it exercises, or "kills," its option to invest. It gives up the possibility of waiting for new information to arrive that might affect the desirability or timing of the expenditure; it cannot disinvest should market conditions change adversely. This lost option value is an opportunity cost that must be included as part of the cost of the investment.   (page 6)

According to the authors, this opportunity cost can be quite large, and its omission from "traditional" methods of capital budgeting explains the gap between existing theory and observed behaviour in practise. Like much of modern financial theory, this method of capital budgeting has yet to work its way from the arcane playing fields of the theoretician into the toolbox of the practitioner.

7.   Investment Appraisal: Risk

The notion of risk pervades all existence. Benjamin Franklin is often quoted as having said, "The only things in life which are certain are death and taxes"; and yet even these are uncertain as to their timing and magnitude respectively. Indeed, it might accurately be argued that the only thing in life which is certain is uncertainty!

All human decision-making involves some element of taking risk into consideration, and everyday acts involve some form of recognition of risk. When we cross the road we explicitly acknowledge the risks involved by looking for oncoming traffic before crossing, thereby trying to minimise our risk of death or injury. When purchasing groceries we tend to consider risk implicitly, by assuming that the foods bought will be safe, or that their safety is guaranteed by some authoritative organisation. So it is inevitable that in considering human decision-making in the corporate sphere we need to recognise the role of risk explicitly.

In Chapter Six we examined the process of capital investment appraisal. This involved the firm weighing up the relative costs and benefits of undertaking a given capital investment. Because these benefits and costs take place in an unknown future, they can be only estimates; the actual values will probably differ from those estimates. Thus there is an element of risk to the process of capital budgeting. Additionally, each capital investment has its own inherent risk. These risks must be fully reflected in the magnitude of the cost of capital applied in a Net Present Value appraisal of the investment. In this chapter we consider the explicit consideration of risk in a more scientific manner.

In Chapter Four we saw how an interest rate (or "yield") incorporates an element to compensate lenders for different kinds of risk. Thus, via interest rates the financial markets have a mechanism for 'pricing' risk. Consequently, to understand risk we need to consider it from the objective overview of the financial marketplace, rather than from the subjective perspective of the single corporate entity. This means that in addition to our examination of the marketplace as a financial intermediary, we also need to consider the activities of all of the participants. In Chapters Eight and Nine we will add to our knowledge with a detailed consideration of the demand side of the market for corporate funding. The remainder of this chapter is devoted to a consideration of the activities of the suppliers of funds: investors.

In the case of an (initial) offering by a corporation, investors are supplying funds to that corporation by purchasing the securities offered. This may be via the purchase of shares upon a company's flotation, or the purchase of corporate debt in the primary market. In either case, the primary aim of the investor is to earn a return on their funds, but with an eye to the level of risk involved. This is as true for the individual investor as it is for the professional fund manager.

In everything that follows in this chapter, there is an underlying assumption that the market is efficient (see Section 2.2.2), with all the associated ramifications.

7.1   Risk and Return

Perhaps the most fundamental truism in the entire canon of finance is that represented by the risk-return trade-off. This suggests that the "price" of an investor desiring a higher expected return is the assumption of greater levels of risk. Lower risk involves the acceptance of lower levels of expected return. Thus, the two main characteristics of any financial asset will be its expected return (or yield) and its risk. The securities that are chosen to make up a portfolio will be selected on the basis of their yield and risk characteristics.

7.1.1   Yield (or expected return)
A financial claim may be defined as a contract typically carrying an obligation on the issuer to make periodic payments (e.g., interest, or dividends) and to redeem the claim at a stated value in any one of three ways:

1. on demand;
2. after a stated period of notice has been given; or
3. on a given date or within a given range of dates.

Of course, it is entirely possible (allowable) for one of the forms of payment to take the value of zero. One example might be the shares in a company which does not normally pay dividends (preferring to retain the profits for reinvestment within the firm).

The future periodic payments as well as that on redemption may be fixed or variable in value. For example, a bond may have a fixed rate of interest over its life and a fixed redemption value ("par") stated in advance. Alternatively, the interest may be paid at a variable rate. For example, with an ordinary share in a listed company neither payment is fixed: dividends (the periodic payments) fluctuate according to the proportion of available profits which the directors decide to distribute to shareholders; the redemption value depends upon the market price of the share at the time of sale, or by a share of the realised assets should the company be wound up. Similarly, a deposit with a bank or building society possesses a fixed face value sum on redemption but a varying level of interest payments.

For a contractual right to receive either or both of these forms of future payment to rank as a financial claim the promise to pay must be unconditional. For this reason items such as a life insurance policy deserve the title of a "financial claim" because it promises a given payment upon death or the prior attainment of a certain date. This is not the case with fire insurance, for example, where payment only occurs in the event of fire breaking out, which may not happen. Some contractual obligations to make future payments are not regarded as financial assets because they are not transferable from one owner to another. The payment of a wage or salary under a contract comes into this category.

The yield of a financial asset is the sum total of all expected future periodic payments and the redemption payment. This gives a measure of the absolute return on any financial asset. However, an investor will usually be more concerned with the value of their expected return relative to the purchase price of the asset, i.e., its rate of return. Expressed simply, the percentage rate of return (or yield) of an asset is found using:

$$\text{rate of return} = \frac{\text{receipt} - \text{expenditure}}{\text{expenditure}}$$

where *receipt* is the sum of all future payments, both periodic and redemption, and *expenditure* refers to the purchase price of the asset. Typically these values are unknown except in the present and the past, thus in formulating investment plans the *expected* rate of return is calculated and utilised. If the expected rate of return is positive then it would appear beneficial to purchase the particular financial asset (assuming transactions costs to be negligible, or zero), but this is not the whole story. If an investor can calculate the expected rates of return on all financial assets they can then be ranked according to their expected rates of return. At first glance it would seem reasonable to invest solely in the asset offering the highest expected rate of return, but this would indeed be most unwise. This is because the risk of a financial asset—its second characteristic—must be taken into account in formulating investment selection strategy.

As previously noted, for investors to be induced to accept greater risk they must be compensated with greater expected rates of return, reflecting higher risk premiums. Consequently, we would expect to find a positive relationship between the expected return on an asset and its level of risk. This relationship might best be represented by the following equation:

$$k = r_f + \theta$$

where k is the expected return (or required rate of return, cost of capital), r_f is the risk-free rate of return, and θ is the risk premium. A simple graphical illustration of this relationship would be as follows:

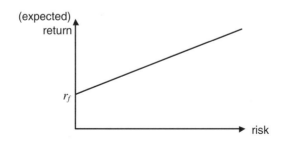

7.1.2   Risk and uncertainty

While the yield on any (financial) asset is a fairly unambiguous concept, it is more difficult to determine exactly what is meant by risk. In much of the literature the term "risk" is used interchangeably with the term "uncertainty", although they are by no means synonymous. The definitions first put forward by Frank Knight [1921] and John Maynard Keynes [1921] have been largely accepted since. Thus, the outcome of a decision is defined as involving "risk" if the probability of (considerable) loss is not small. The outcome of a decision is defined as "uncertain" if:

1. the various pairs of possible outcomes are difficult to compare; or
2. it is difficult to decide on a list of possible outcomes.

Consequently, for situations of risk there exists a well-defined probability (density) function, while uncertainty implies that such a function is ill-defined, if it exists at all.

For Nobel Laureate Milton Friedman it is always possible to turn a situation of "uncertainty" into one of "risk" by assuming that the probability function is known at least subjectively. The apparent interchangeability of the terms "risk" and "uncertainty" is typically based upon this view. It is one with which Keynes was very much at odds, especially in his later writings; referring to "uncertainty" he argues

> The sense in which I am using the term is that in which the prospect of a European war is uncertain, or the price of copper and the rate of interest twenty years hence, or the obsolescence of a new invention, or the position of private wealth-owners in the social system in 1970. About these matters there is no scientific basis on which to form any capable probability whatever. We simply do not know.   (1937, page 217)

Because of the large amount of time-series data available on securities it can be argued that capital markets can be regarded as situations of "risk"; the volumes of historic data give rise to a set of probabilities for a large number of possible outcomes. It is largely on this basis that probability theory is used for modelling the impact of risk and (expected) return on investment behaviour.

It should be noted that the risk attached to any financial claim is not immutable. In part this is because the financial system is a highly dynamic sector of the economy, with intermediaries constantly seeking to innovate either to evade legislative constraints or to improve upon the competition. Thus, for example, with the appearance of new financial markets and the increased competition due to more trading on older markets, many financial assets experience diminishing marketability risk over time. It would certainly seem to be the case that increasing internationalisation of the world's capital markets coupled with sensible deregulation should lead to higher potential returns for investors (partly in terms of a wider range of alternatives) as well as a diminution of risk within most of the various categories, as well as because of the possibility of increased geographic portfolio diversification.

7.1.2   Risk and probability

Most people in considering risk tend to focus on the possibility of loss; that is to say "downside risk". Scientifically, risk deals with the probability of divergence from some "normal" or "expected" value. This divergence should include both downside risk (the risk of loss) as well as any "upside potential" (the risk of gain). To quantify risk we begin by defining the expected return of an economic variable, $E(R)$, as a weighted average of all of the possible returns, where the weights used are the relevant probabilities:

$$E(R) = \sum p_i r_i$$

This weighted average, or "expected return", is also referred to as the "mean" of the distribution; μ or $\overline{R}$ in notation.

Example:

For a stake (outlay) of £1,500, Ardiles Lotteries offers the chance of four possible prizes (outcomes) with the following corresponding probabilities:

outcome number	return, R	probability, p	p * R
1	£1,000	0.1	£100
2	£2,000	0.2	£400
3	£3,000	0.4	£1,200
4	£4,000	0.3	£1,200
		$\sum p = 1.0$	E(R) = £2,900

Thus, an outlay of £1,500 has an expected return of £2,900, which seems attractive at first glance. More normally the returns will be *rates of return*, expressed as a percentage, thus we might typically see:

outcome number	rate of return, r	probability, p	p * r
1	−0.05 or −5%	0.1	-0.005
2	0.02 or 2%	0.2	0.004
3	0.05 or 5%	0.4	0.02
4	0.07 or 7%	0.3	0.021
		$\sum p = 1.0$	E(r) = 0.04 or 4%

However, this ignores the element of risk, which is quantified by the dispersion of the returns. This can be plotted as a probability distribution. Using our original example we find:

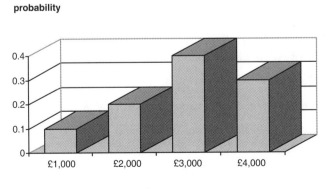

Of course, in reality there are usually more than four possible outcomes for a given economic variable, such as the return on a security. When there are a large number of possible outcomes the probability distribution will tend to look less discrete—more continuous—like the following:

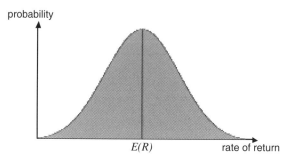

Most finance theory is predicated upon the assumption that the rate of return on a financial asset traded in an efficient market (such as equity, or government and corporate bonds) is normally distributed, as shown in the diagram above. The lower the risk, the narrower will be the dispersion; the higher the risk, the flatter and more dispersed will be the curve. In the extreme, a *certain* outcome (one with probability of 100%) will be portrayed by a single vertical line at its certain expected value, $E(R)$, going up to 100% probability.

The dispersion of a probability distribution is quantified by making use of the statistical measure of standard deviation, σ.

$$\sigma = \sqrt{\sum_j p_j \left[R_j - E(R_j) \right]^2}$$

While quite daunting at first glance, this formula can be broken down into a series of calculations, each of which is quite straightforward taken individually:

1. calculate the expected return, $E(R) \equiv \overline{R} \equiv \mu$

2. calculate the deviation of each possible return from the mean, $R_j - E(R)$

3. calculate the square of each deviation from the mean, $[R_j - E(R)]^2$

4. multiply each squared deviation by its probability, $p_j[R_j - E(R)]^2$
5. add these last up: $\sum p_j[R_j - E(R)]^2$
6. find the square root of this sum.

This is best done by use of a simple table of calculations. Using data from the previous example:

R_i	p_i	$R_i - E(R)$	$[R_i - E(R)]^2$	$p_i[R_i - E(R)]^2$
£1,000	0.1	-1,900	3,610,000	361,000
£2,000	0.2	-900	810,000	162,000
£3,000	0.4	100	10,000	4,000
£4,000	0.3	1,100	1,210,000	363,000
			variance $\Rightarrow \sum$ =	890,000

The variance of the distribution is 890,000; the standard deviation (the square root of the variance) is 943.40. This provides a measure of the risk of this particular lottery. A lottery (or a security) with the same expected return and a higher standard deviation would be considered more risky, and thus less attractive to a rational investor. Of course, in the case of a "fair lottery" or a financial asset it is typically the case that a security with higher risk will offer a higher expected return, as we shall see.

7.2 Portfolio theory: The Markowitz Approach

The foregoing provides a means of comparing individual securities (or risky cash flows, returns on assets, etc.) by using the statistical measures of mean (μ) and variance (or standard deviation, σ). However, experience and observation tells us that most investors do not purchase a single asset, preferring instead a basket of securities, known as a portfolio. At its most oversimplified, the results of portfolio theory are little more than homage to the time-honoured adage to avoid "putting all one's eggs into one basket". While the wisdom for holding a diversified portfolio of assets is almost as old as time, it was only with the pioneering work of Harry Markowitz [1952, 1959] and A. D. Roy [1958] that a sound theoretical explanation for such behaviour was provided. It follows from their work that any consideration of a portfolio needs to take into account that there may be some interaction between the characteristics of the individual assets held in the portfolio. Consider the following example of mean-variance (μ-σ) characteristics:

	Mean, μ	Variance, σ^2	standard deviation, σ
Asset A	0.20	0.2476	0.0613
Asset B	0.13	0.2433	0.0592

As expected, Asset A has both a higher expected return (mean) and a higher risk (as measured both by its standard deviation and its variance). At first glance, this might seem to suggest that the best investment strategy would be to invest all of one's monies in Asset A; that there is little to gain by combining it with Asset B in a portfolio. But, further analysis proves to be revealing as we discover below.

7.2.1   Portfolio returns

The expected return on a portfolio of assets is simply a weighted average of the expected returns on each of the individual securities. The weights are the proportions of the portfolio accounted for by each security, which must sum to one. Thus:

$$\mu_p \equiv E(R_p) = \omega_A \mu_A + \omega_B \mu_B + \omega_C \mu_C + \ldots$$

where ω_A is the proportion of Asset A in the portfolio (thus $\Sigma \omega_i = 1$), and μ_A is the expected return on asset A. Alternatively, using summation notation:

$$\mu_p = E(R_p) = \sum_{i=1}^{N} \omega_i \mu_i$$

Example:

Consider a two-asset portfolio consisting of £150m worth of Asset A and £25m worth of Asset B. Thus, $\omega_A = 75\%$ and $\omega_B = 25\%$. The expected return on this portfolio will be:

$$\mu_p \equiv E(R_p) = (0.75)(0.20) + (0.25)(0.13) = 0.1825$$

i.e., 18.25%.

Similarly, for a portfolio made up of 50% asset A and 50% asset B the expected return would be:

$$\mu_p \equiv E(R_p) = (0.5)(0.20) + (0.5)(0.13) = 0.165$$

i.e., 16.5%.

Note that regardless of the weights, the expected return on the portfolio lies somewhere between the two individual asset expected returns. This confirms the notion that based solely on returns, a portfolio consisting entirely of Asset A would be preferred. But this would be to neglect the risk factor, the possible variance in expected returns.

7.2.2 Portfolio risk

Intuition might suggest that the risk of a portfolio is a weighted average of the individual risks pertaining to the assets held in the portfolio. But this would be only partially correct. The risk on a portfolio of assets is more difficult to calculate, being based on a (seemingly) complex formula. However, in general terms the portfolio risk depends only on a few variables: the risk of each individual security (its standard deviation, σ); the proportion of each security held in the portfolio (ϖ); and the relationship between the various securities as measured by the covariance between their returns. Thus, for a simple two-asset portfolio, the risk appears as:

$$\sigma_p = \sqrt{\left(\varpi_A^2 \sigma_A^2 + \varpi_B^2 \sigma_B^2 + 2\varpi_A \varpi_B Cov_{AB}\right)}$$

where σ_p is the standard deviation of the portfolio, ϖ_A represents the proportion of asset A held in the portfolio, σ_A is the risk of asset A as measured by its standard deviation of returns, and Cov_{AB} is the covariance of the returns between asset A and asset B. The covariance is a measure of the degree to which the returns on the two assets move together, and is therefore related to the correlation coefficient, ρ, between the returns on any two assets:

$$Cov_{AB} = \sigma_i\sigma_j\rho_{ij}$$

By selecting assets with low correlation of returns it is feasible to reduce the overall risk of the portfolio. This occurs because as the returns on one asset go down they will be offset by the returns on another asset going up, keeping the overall return on the portfolio stable; that is to say, with a low degree of variation. This is more likely to occur with securities from firms in different industries, especially if those industries move differently against the macroeconomic business cycle (e.g. one moves with the cycle, the other counter-cyclically).

Example:

You have recently had the good fortune to receive a financial windfall. After careful consideration of all the options, you have decided to purchase a small portfolio of shares. You have been impressed with the performance of two companies in particular—Greaves International plc and Chivers plc—and are planning a two-asset portfolio consisting of shares in those companies, which have the following characteristics:

	Asset A (Greaves Int.)	Asset B (Chivers plc)
μ	0.12	0.08
σ	0.09	0.06
ω	50%	50%

Given that you plan to allocate half of your portfolio to each asset ($\omega_A = \omega_B = 50\%$), what level of risk will you be assuming?

Suppose that the correlation coefficient (ρ_{AB}) between the individual asset returns was 1.0; that is to say, the asset returns were perfectly correlated. Then the standard deviation of the portfolio would be

$$\sigma_p = [(0.5)^2(0.09)^2 + (0.5)^2(0.06)^2 + 2(0.5)(0.5)Cov_{AB}]^{1/2}$$

Because $Cov_{AB} = \rho_{AB}\sigma_A\sigma_B$, the standard deviation is

$$\sigma_p = [(0.5)^2(0.09)^2 + (0.5)^2(0.06)^2 + 2(0.5)(0.5)(1.0)(0.09)(0.06)]^{1/2}$$

$$\sigma_p = 0.075$$

Note that this combination offers a lower level of risk to the investor than that for Greaves International ($\sigma = 0.09$), but which is marginally higher than that for Chivers plc ($\sigma = 0.06$). Of course, in practice it is very unlikely to be able to find two assets with perfectly correlated returns to combine in a portfolio. Indeed, what the rational investor would ideally be seeking would be two assets with a negative correlation between the returns on the two assets.

Consider what would have occurred in the previous example had the correlation coefficient, ρ_{AB}, had been -0.2. Then the standard deviation of returns on the two-asset portfolio would turn out to be 0.0488, which implies a lower level of risk for the portfolio itself than for either of the individual assets of which the portfolio is composed.

A similar pattern emerges if the correlation coefficient is lower than one, but remains positive. For example, if the value of ρ_{AB} was 0.1 a standard deviation of 0.0565 emerges. This is still lower than the risk for either of the two assets individually.

If we plot a graph of the standard deviation (risk) which results from possible values for the correlation coefficient between individual investment returns in the previous example, a positive relationship between them emerges:

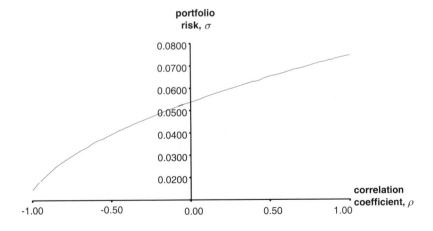

We can see that there is a distinct inverse relationship between the risk of the portfolio and the correlation coefficient between the returns on the two assets in the portfolio. Another way of considering this same relationship is via a graph in risk-return (mean-standard deviation) space:

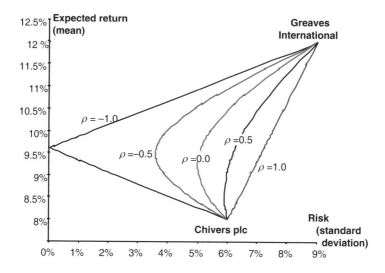

Unsurprisingly, the same principle also exists for a multiple-asset portfolio, where the general formula for portfolio risk, σ_p, is given by:

$$\sigma_p = \sqrt{\sum_{i=1}^{N} \sum_{j=1}^{N} \omega_i \omega_j \sigma_i \sigma_j \rho_{ij}}$$

where ω_i represents the proportion of the portfolio invested in asset i, σ_i is the standard deviation of returns on asset i, and $-1 \leq \rho \leq +1$. This may be expressed more clearly as:

$$\sigma_p = \sqrt{\sum_{i=1}^{N} \omega_i^2 \sigma_i^2 + 2\sum_{j=1}^{N-1} \sum_{i=j+1}^{N} \omega_i \omega_j \sigma_i \sigma_j \rho_{ij}}$$

Example:

You are considering investing in a portfolio consisting of three securities with the following characteristics:

P_s	Rate of Return on		
	Security 1	**Security 2**	**Security 3**
0.1	0.25	0.25	0.1
0.4	0.2	0.15	0.15
0.4	0.15	0.2	0.2
0.1	0.1	0.1	0.25

It follows that the expected return on each of these three securities will be as follows:

$$\mu_1 = 17.5\%, \ \mu_2 = 17.5\%, \ \mu_3 = 17.5\%$$

Similarly, using the formulas already explained, the risk for each of these securities as measured by its standard deviation is:

$$\sigma_1 = 4.03112\%, \ \sigma_2 = 4.03112\%, \ \sigma_3 = 4.03112\%$$

It would seem, therefore, that there is little to choose between these three securities as they each have the same risk/return characteristics. Intuition suggests that your portfolio will be the same regardless of how it is composed of these three securities. However, unless your portfolio were to consist entirely of any one of these securities alone, intuition would be incorrect. While the expected return of a portfolio of any combination of these assets would always yield 17.5 per cent, the risk would differ.

Consider the portfolio consisting one-quarter of Security 1, one-quarter of Security 3, and one-half of Security 2. The expected return of this portfolio would be

$$\mu_p = (0.25 * \mu_1) + (0.5 * \mu_2) + (0.25 * \mu_3)$$

$$\mu_p = (0.25 * 0.175) + (0.5 * 0.175) + (0.25 * 0.175) = 17.5\%$$

The covariances between the returns on these assets calculate as:

$$cov_{12} = 0.000625, \quad cov_{13} = -0.001625, \quad cov_{23} = -0.000625$$

Using these covariances, the risk attached to this portfolio would be as follows:

$$\sigma_p = \sqrt{\sum_{i=1}^{N} \varpi_i^2 \sigma_i^2 + 2\sum_{j=1}^{N-1} \sum_{i=j+1}^{N} \varpi_i \varpi_j cov_{ij}}$$

$\sigma_p^2 = [(0.25^2*0.040311^2) + (0.5^2*0.040311^2) + (0.25^2*0.040311^2)] +$

$2* [(0.25*0.5*0.000625) + (0.5*0.25* -0.000625) + (0.25*0.25* -0.001625)]$

$\sigma_p = 2.016\ \%$

Thus, the risk of a portfolio consisting of all three assets is lower than any of the individual asset risks. In large part, this is due to the negative covariances between the returns of asset 2 and asset 3 and between asset 1 and asset 3.

Had we split the portfolio equally between the three securities, with each accounting for one-third, the risk of the portfolio turns out even lower, at 1.344%.

The implications of the example are quite clear. In order to minimise the risk accruing to any portfolio it is important to identify and include securities whose returns are (ideally) negatively correlated with those of existing securities in the portfolio. Once these securities have been identified, they should be combined in proportions which serves to minimise the risk, *ceteris paribus*. One way to consider this is via a simple "thought experiment": imagine that you have a portfolio consisting of a single asset. This provides you with an expected return and a level of risk commensurate with those of the single asset *per se*.

In order to reduce (minimise) risk through diversification, you now seek to add a second asset to the portfolio. It should be a task of relative ease to find a second asset with returns which are negatively correlated with those of the asset already in your portfolio (such as from a company in a different industry, for example). We have already seen how this will serve to reduce the level of risk of the portfolio below that of either of the two assets of which it is comprised.

You then seek to diversify further by the addition of a third asset, which should have returns negatively correlated with those of the two assets already in your portfolio; this should be possible, but not as easy as finding the previous (second) asset. This was illustrated in the last example.

To further minimise risk via diversification you need to add an additional asset with returns negatively correlated with the pre-existing assets in the portfolio. The more of these latter there are, the more difficult it becomes to meet the criteria of negative correlation of returns. Thus, the more difficult it becomes to lower risk by the further addition of assets to the portfolio. Graphically this appears as:

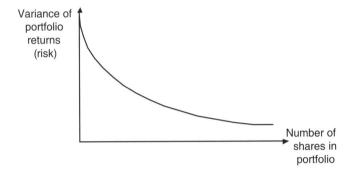

Note that the risk level as measured by the variance never quite reaches zero!

In summary, the Markowitz approach offers a good explanation of the phenomenon of portfolio risk-reduction through diversification. However, it is not entirely practicable, as it requires calculating the correlation coefficient between the returns on all possible pairs of assets! One way round this is to introduce a common measure against which each individual asset's risk might be measured. Such a common measure might be a single benchmark security, or a benchmark portfolio. One such benchmark portfolio might be the market portfolio: a portfolio consisting of every security available, in proportion to their overall availability. "Every security available" should include securities of every description, including ordinary shares, preference shares, bonds, warrants, convertible bonds, and so on. If the ordinary shares issued by a given company represented 0.037% of the value of equity of all companies, the market portfolio's equity sector should also contain 0.037% of that share.

7.3   Market Risk

Let us now turn our attention specifically to market-traded investments, such as equity stocks. Movements in share prices, and hence their rates of return, can be related to two major sources:

1. *unsystematic information.* This is share-specific or company-specific, and hence includes information that will tend to affect the company alone. Such information might include an increased level of company profits, the death of the firm's key owner (especially if a charismatic figure or a person of great renown), the possibility of a takeover bid, or firm-specific industrial action.
2. *systematic information.* This is general market-wide information that tends to affect all companies, albeit to differing degrees, and not necessarily in the same direction. For example, macroeconomic policy changes—such as changes in interest rates, or changes in the tax regime—would come under this category.

Thus, for any given security, such as an ordinary share, we may define the following:

$$(\text{Risk of a share}) = (\text{systematic risk}) + (\text{unsystematic risk})$$

or, less formally:

$$(\text{Risk of a share}) = (\text{Share market risk}) + (\text{Share} - \text{specific risk})$$

Similarly, for a portfolio:

$$\begin{pmatrix} \text{Risk of} \\ \text{a portfolio} \end{pmatrix} = \begin{pmatrix} \text{systematic risk} \\ \text{(Share market risk)} \end{pmatrix} + \begin{pmatrix} \text{unsystematic risk} \\ \text{(Portfolio-specific risk)} \end{pmatrix}$$

By means of portfolio diversification it is possible to reduce the risk occasioned by unsystematic information; that is to say, unsystematic risk can be reduced by diversification. Systematic risk is essentially market-wide risk, and cannot be reduced by diversification. The only exception to this is via geographical diversification into other markets. However, in such a case the systematic risk applies *globally*, and not simply to the local market. Local market "systematic" risk can be considered as another form of unsystematic risk.

For reasons explained in the previous section, in practice there is likely to be a limit to the reduction of risk via such diversification that can be achieved by a (equity-only) portfolio. Indeed, studies have revealed the following phenomenon:

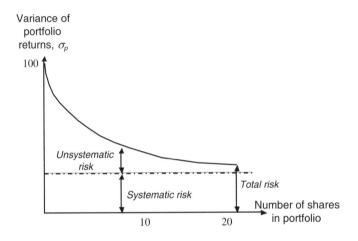

Thus, although the unsystematic risk for an individual share may be quite substantial, it may be reduced considerably (possibly to zero!) by diversification within a portfolio. The diagram above shows what various studies have revealed: that this may be achieved with a portfolio of between fifteen and twenty appropriately selected shares, which is a relatively small number of securities. It also illustrates the relationship that exists between the risk for a given portfolio and the risk pertaining to the market as a whole. It is this relationship that we now consider, via the statistic specifically designed to measure it.

7.3.1 The beta coefficient (β)

The beta coefficient, β, is a measure of the **relative systematic risk** of a share. It measures the risk of a security relative to the market portfolio. The beta coefficient, therefore, offers us the single benchmark we seek for easy comparison of a security's risk; it is no longer necessary to calculate the correlation coefficient of returns between each and every possible security combination. It is defined as

$$\beta_j = \frac{Cov(r_j, r_M)}{Var(r_M)} \equiv \frac{Cov_{jM}}{Var_M}$$

where r_M indicates returns on the market portfolio, thus $Var(r_M)$ is the variance of market returns, and $Cov(r_j, r_M)$ is the covariance between returns on security j and returns on the market portfolio, M. The beta coefficient (β) is sometimes described as a measure of security j's contribution to overall market risk.

More fully, we may define the beta coefficient as follows:

$$\beta_j = \frac{Cov(r_j, r_M)}{Var(r_M)} = \frac{\rho_{jm}\sigma_j}{\sigma_m}$$

or alternatively
$$\beta_j = \frac{E\left[r_j * r_M\right] - E\left[r_j\right] * E\left[r_M\right]}{E\left[r_M^2\right] - E\left[r_M\right]^2}$$

Bearing in mind the inverse relationship between the price of a share and its rate of return (see Chapter 5), there are three key possibilities for the value of β:

$\beta_j = 1$ Security j's returns will behave exactly as the returns on the market portfolio

$\beta_j > 1$ Security j's returns are more volatile than those on the market; if the return on the market portfolio goes up, security j's return also rises but in a greater proportion

$\beta_j < 1$ Security j's returns are less volatile than those on the market; if the return on the market portfolio goes up, the return on security j rises to a lesser degree.

    One special case in this range occurs when $\beta = 0$. Then the returns on the security are perfectly uncorrelated with the market's return, thus the security has no market-related risk.

It therefore follows that an investor who wished to follow ("track") the market should select a portfolio of securities with beta coefficient values close to one. If the market generally is in a "bull phase" with share prices rising, then (on average) capital gains might be found by investing in securities with beta coefficients greater than one. Of course, this implies taking a greater risk for a potentially higher return. The risk-averse investor will typically prefer to hold a portfolio of securities with low beta coefficients.

In practice β coefficients are calculated using historical data, typically using monthly observations over the previous five years. The data are used to estimate the total return—including dividends and any capital gain or loss—from investing in a security and in the relevant market index. These returns are then regressed against each other and the slope of the resulting regression line gives the beta coefficient (β). Graphically, this relationship appears:

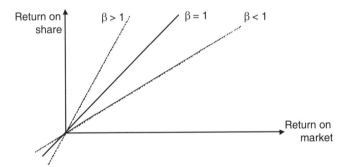

The regression equation for this relationship is of the form (ignoring the possible error term):

$$r_j = \alpha + \beta_j * r_M$$

where α is the intercept, and is referred to as the "abnormal return".

Theoretically, α should take the value of zero, however, in practice it often has a value close to zero, but may fluctuate at any time between negative and positive values. An α which is positive implies a "buy" signal; if such a signal is responded to by (many) investors, then the price of the share will rise in response to the increased demand, leading to a reduction in its rate of return, thereby lowering α towards 0; similarly, if α is negative. Thus, arbitrage ensures a value of α close to zero! Of course, the 'success' of such arbitrage in ensuring a value of a close to zero depends on the market being efficient.

Although contemporary computing makes it feasible for the individual to gather data and calculate beta coefficients, there are established providers who sell the results of their calculations. In the USA there is widespread competition among such providers, with highly competitive prices; in the United Kingdom, there is an effective monopoly, with the London Business School publishing a quarterly *Risk Measurement Service* which, in addition to beta coefficients, offers other statistical information on UK companies of any significance.

Because of the relative ease-of-access, as well as the huge volume of data available, most beta coefficients tend to be calculated for the equity market. Indeed, reading some commentators might give the impression that beta coefficients solely apply to equity markets, which is simply not the case. In the United Kingdom, the FT–Actuaries All-Share Index is used as a proxy for the market. The five-year beta is most common, although it is entirely feasible to define a beta measured over a shorter period. Typically betas increase in volatility as the length of the period reduces, although it may more accurately reflect current conditions. Indeed, some companies have been known to supply beta estimates based on five days to provide an extremely short-term view of market conditions!

7.4   The Capital Asset Pricing Model (CAPM)

Before the second half of the twentieth century it was intuitively understood that investor risk could be reduced by holding a diversified portfolio of assets. With the advent of the 1950s, the application of statistical and other quantitative methods to financial behaviour began to offer theoretical insights that had previously been missing. The work of Harry Markowitz [1952, 1959], A. D. Roy [1958], and James Tobin [1958] provided the foundations for modern portfolio theory. These pioneering expositions, while providing a sound theoretical background, could not be exploited practically, as they required each security in a portfolio to be compared with every other possible security in terms of correlation of returns. This drawback was eliminated in the 1960s by the work of William Sharpe, John Lintner and Jan Mossin, which resulted in the Capital Asset Pricing Model. The CAPM provided a simplifying device by comparing each security's return with a single yardstick: the return on the market portfolio *in toto*. This device is the *beta coefficient*. Therefore, the CAPM is a *single-factor model*, depending only upon the securities market.

Under the Capital Asset Pricing Model, it is assumed that

1. the market is efficient, and
2. that investors live in a mean-variance world (i.e. they measure return and risk by mean and variance respectively), with more return preferred to less, and lower risk preferred to higher.

Consequently, it is possible for a range of investments in both individual stocks and (more importantly) portfolios to be plotted in terms of their mean-variance characteristics:

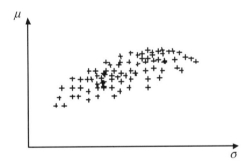

Each + symbol represents a portfolio in terms of its mean-variance characteristics. An **efficient portfolio** is defined as one which has

- highest expected return (μ) for a given risk level (σ), or
- lowest risk (σ) for a given expected return (μ).

Some portfolios, including those consisting of a single-security, will be efficient. Given that investors prefer higher expected returns and lower levels of risk, portfolios which are efficient should dominate those which are inefficient. The locus of efficient portfolios is referred to as the *efficient frontier*.

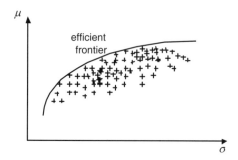

Given the assumption that the market is efficient, then arbitrage will ensure that portfolios with low returns and high risks will be sold, driving their price down and increasing their return. Ultimately all portfolios should lie on the efficient frontier!

If we now introduce the concept of a **risk-free investment** (i.e. one with no variation in its return), which may be held as well as a portfolio of risky assets, then the Efficient Market Line (EML) may be considered:

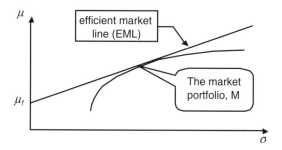

It is possible to achieve any risk-return combination represented by the EML via a portfolio consisting of the risk-free investment and any investment lying on the frontier. This assumes that it is possible to "go short". In theory, because all risky investments should lie on the line, any risky investment would do. In practice a market index portfolio is used as a good all-round average. All stocks with returns below the EML will be sold until the price is driven down, and the return goes up

The equation of the EML may be written as

$$\mu_p = \mu_f + \left(\frac{\mu_m - \mu_f}{\sigma_m} \right) * \sigma_p$$

where p refers to some efficient portfolio, and m indicates the market (index) portfolio. (Note that μ_m-μ_f is referred to as the **market risk premium**, measuring the risk attached to the market portfolio over and above the risk-free rate of return.) This expression should also be true for the market portfolio; thus

$$\mu_m = \mu_f + \left(\frac{\mu_m - \mu_f}{\sigma_m} \right) * \sigma_m$$

Now, the market portfolio consists of a number of stocks such that

$$\mu_m = \sum \omega_i \mu_i \qquad \text{(i.e. weighted average of expected returns)}$$
$$\sigma_m^2 = \sum \omega_i \sigma_{im} \qquad \text{(i.e. weighted sum of covariances)}$$
$$\sum \omega_i = 1 \qquad \text{(i.e. the weights sum to one)}$$

where $\sigma_{im} = \text{covariance}(R_i, M)$. It therefore follows that

$$\sum_i \varpi_i \mu_i = \sum_i \varpi_i \mu_f + \left(\frac{\mu_m - \mu_f}{\sigma_m^2} \right) \sum_i \varpi_i \sigma_{im},$$

or alternatively

$$\sum_i \varpi_i * \left\{ \mu_i - \mu_f + \left(\frac{\mu_m - \mu_f}{\sigma_m^2} \right) * \sigma_{im} \right\} = 0$$

In an efficient market, where individual stocks are bought and sold, the only practical solution to the above equation is:

$$\mu_i - \mu_f + \left(\frac{\mu_m - \mu_f}{\sigma_m^2} \right) * \sigma_{im} = 0$$

for all stocks; or, using the definition of β given above, we derive the **fundamental equation of the Capital Asset Pricing Model:**

$$\mu_i = \mu_f + \left(\mu_m - \mu_f \right) * \beta_i$$

It follows from the foregoing that the expected return on an investment is related to

- a risk-free return (such as 90-day government bills)
- the additional premium the stock market provides over and above the risk-free rate
- the individual variability of each share return relative to the market average

This gives rise to the Securities Market Line:

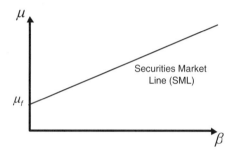

The CAPM is sometimes expressed as

$$\mu_i = \mu_f + \theta_i$$

where θ_i is the risk premium. Thus, if the expected return on the market portfolio (μ_m) is 16%, and μ_f is 7%, then the market risk premium ($\theta_m = \mu_m - \mu_f$) will be 9%. For a security with $\beta = 1$, the risk premium should equal the market risk premium. A security with $\beta = 2$ should be twice as risky as the market average, and so its market risk premium should be twice the market risk premium; thus

$$\theta_i = \left(\mu_m - \mu_f\right) * \beta_i$$

$$\theta_i = (16 - 7)*2 = 18\%$$

and hence, $\mu_i = 7\% + 18\% = 25\%$ as a pre-tax target.

The importance of CAPM as part of modern financial theory should not be underestimated. While the underlying assumptions are quite rigorous (and some would argue unrealistic) it goes a long way to providing an explanatory framework for relating risk and return. As we shall see, such a framework provides a useful tool for considering many situations.

Finally, when calculating the beta of a portfolio, this is the weighted average of the betas of the individual shares, where the weights reflect the asset values:

$$\beta_p = \Sigma \omega_i \beta_i$$

where β_p = the portfolio beta, β_i represents the betas for the individual shares, and ω_i represents the appropriate weights.

7.4.1 Value additivity

A company can readily be described as a portfolio of the (real) investment projects it undertakes. Suppose a company consists of two such projects, A and B. Hence, the market value of the firm will be PV(A + B) = PV(A) + PV(B). This may seem a little too obvious so, using CAPM, assume that

- each project lasts for one year and generates a cash flow of £100 at the end of the year
- project A has a β of 1.0 and project B has a β of 2
- the risk-free rate (R_f) is 10% *per annum*, and the market risk premium (R_m - R_f) is 8% *per annum*

The desired (expected) return on A will be $\mu_A = R_f + (R_m - R_f)^*\beta_A = 10\% + (8\%^*1) = 18\%$; and $\mu_B = 26\%$. Thus:

$$PV(A) = \frac{£100}{(1 + \mu_A)} = \frac{£100}{(1.18)} = £84.75; \text{ and } PV(B) = £79.37$$

Using value additivity, PV(A + B) = £84.75 + £79.37 = £164.12. Alternatively, using the CAPM, one can first calculate the β of (A+B) using a weighted average:

$$\beta_{A+B} = \beta_A * \left[\frac{PV(A)}{PV(A + B)} \right] + \beta_B * \left[\frac{PV(B)}{PV(A + B)} \right] = 1.484$$

Secondly, calculate the expected return:

$$\mu_{A+B} \;=\; R_f \;+\; \left(R_m \;-\; R_f\right)^* \beta_{A+B} \;=\; 21.87\%$$

And finally, calculate the present value:

$$PV(A+B) \;=\; \frac{200}{\left(1 + \mu_{A+B}\right)} \;=\; 164.12$$

7.5   Arbitrage Pricing Theory

While the CAPM offers both theoretical and practical insights beyond those of its progenitor, the Markowitz approach, it is certainly not immune to criticism. There have been substantial criticisms concerning the credibility of its underlying assumptions. Such assumptions include the probability distribution of returns being normal, or the rather technical condition that investors have quadratic utility functions. Additionally, CAPM is dependent upon there being a market portfolio of all risky assets; indeed, the market portfolio is the foundation on which CAPM is built. Also, the difficulty of finding a reasonably accurate proxy for the risk-free rate of return, r_f, should not be underestimated, despite the increasing institutionalisation of the rate on Treasury bills as such. Empirical studies have found that beta coefficients for individual securities tend not to be stable, while those for portfolios were for long enough sample periods and adequate trading volume. One response to these criticisms was for academics to offer an alternative asset pricing theory which requires only limited, credible assumptions, and yet which would also be regarded as intuitive. This resulted in the development of the Arbitrage Pricing Theory (APT) by Stephen Ross [1976].

Whereas the CAPM is a *single-factor model*, relating the expected return on a stock (or portfolio) to the market portfolio alone, APT is a *multi-factor model*, which effectively includes the CAPM as a special case. In addition to the market portfolio, APT makes use of an advanced statistical technique known as "factor analysis" to identify other factors which affect the pricing of a security.

APT is built on three main assumptions:

1. perfect capital markets
2. investors prefer more wealth to less wealth under certainty
3. the stochastic process generating asset returns can be represented by a (linear) k-factor model as

$$R_j = E_j + b_{j1}F_1 + b_{j2}F_2 + b_{j3}F_3 + ... + b_{jk}F_k + \varepsilon_j$$

for all $j = 1 ... N$, where:

R_j is the return on asset j,

E_j is the expected return on asset j,

F_k represents factor scores,

b_{jk} represents the reaction of asset j's returns to movements in F_k,

ε_j represents a unique effect on asset j's returns, and

N is the number of assets.

In summary, APT suggests that the returns on any given asset will be determined by a series of factors which are common to all assets (systematic factors, represented by F_k), and by factors unique to the given asset (unsystematic factors, represented by ε_j). It is assumed that F are uncorrelated both with each other and with ε_j, and that the means of F and ε are zero.

Because investors are considered to be rational, they will choose to hold a diversified portfolio to eliminate risk via ε_j. Market equilibrium will occur when arbitrage will no longer yield better returns or lower risk. At this point, the expected return on asset j would take the form

$$E_j = R_f + b_{j1}(F_1 - R_f) + b_{j2}(F_2 - R_f) + ... + b_{jk}(F_k - R_f)$$

where R_f is the risk-free rate of return, and the $(F_i - R_f)$ represent the risk premiums with respect to the common factors identified (see below).

By looking explicitly at common factors, APT recognises that some stocks will be more sensitive to particular factors than others, and avoids the CAPM assumption that this is all taken care of within the return on the market portfolio. However, APT is dependent on accurate determination of the relevant factors via (e.g.) factor analysis. Various empirical studies have concluded that these factors tend to be macroeconomic, with the four most important being (unanticipated) changes in

- inflation
- industrial production
- the term structure of interest rates, and
- the default risk premium on bonds.

The resulting multi-factor model can be used to create portfolios that track a market index, or to estimate and monitor the risk of an asset allocation strategy, and even to estimate the probable response of a portfolio to economic developments.

Tests of the APT have shown it to provide a superior explanation to CAPM of historical rates of return on securities. Nonetheless, its usefulness in the practical arena is limited, primarily because of the difficulty of using four explanatory factors (as opposed to the one of the CAPM).

In the next chapter we examine one practical use of the CAPM; to calculate the cost of equity capital.

8.   The Cost of Capital

8.1   Overview

Probably the most important concept in the entire canon of finance is *valuation*, both in theory and in practice. Anything that consists of a stream of cash flows can be considered for valuation. We have already considered the valuation of the firm, equity, debt, and investment projects. We made extensive use of the Net Present Value concept for valuation purposes. For NPV to work requires knowledge of an appropriate discount rate, which is usually determined in the financial marketplace. To the provider of funds this discount rate represents a *required rate of return*; to the corporation seeking funds, this discount rate represents its *cost of capital*. At its broadest, the cost of capital to the firm represents the cost of acquiring or using funds. Naturally, cost refers to *opportunity cost*. More narrowly there are a number of ways of defining the cost of capital, including:

- the minimum return expected by an investor in order to remain in an existing investment (or be tempted into a new one)
- the minimum rate of return which the firm must earn on its new investments to cover its investment costs.

8.2   Sources of Capital

The funding for a company's investments may be acquired from either internal or external sources. Traditionally, three major sources are recognised:

- equity
- debt
- retained earnings

where the latter is internal, and the former two are external sources. For very large investments the company may need to raise specific fresh funding. For most purposes a company would consider having a pool of funds for investment, without breaking down the sources. Nonetheless, the different sources of capital will typically have different costs, which should be calculated on an after-tax basis. We now consider these individually, before progressing to consider the firm's overall (or weighted average) cost of capital.

8.3   The Cost of Debt

At its simplest, the cost of debt is the cost incurred by the firm when it acquires funds through borrowing. In a very real sense, if a firm can borrow funds at 9 per cent, then by definition its *component cost of debt* is 9 per cent. Thus, for example, if a firm borrows £100,000 for one year, paying the suppliers of those funds £9,000 annual interest, then:

$$k_d = \frac{interest}{principal} = \frac{£9,000}{£100,000} = 9\%$$

However, this ignores certain complicating factors, such as multi-year borrowing and corporate taxation. Where funds are borrowed on a multi-year basis, the cost of debt can readily be calculated using the bond valuation formula (see Section 4.2):

$$P_0 = \sum_{t=1}^{T} \frac{c_t}{\left(1+k_d\right)^t} + \frac{M}{\left(1+k_d\right)^t}$$

where c_t is the coupon payment at time t, M is the capital (principal) repayment at maturity, and P_0 is the issue price (or money raised). The yield-to-maturity, k_d, (also known as the redemption yield, or IRR) is the cost of debt. This can also be rewritten as follows, using the annuity formula for the coupon payments:

$$P_0 = c\left[\frac{1}{k_d} - \frac{1}{k_d(1+k_d)^t}\right] + \frac{M}{\left(1+k_d\right)^t}$$

This approach easily incorporates many kinds of debt, including discount, and may even be extended to include embedded option structures as well.

Because interest is typically paid out before tax, it is neccesary to adjust the cost of debt. One way is to estimate the after-tax cost of debt, k_d^* as

$$k_d^* = k_d(1-\tau)$$

where k_d is the pre-tax cost of debt, calculated as above, and τ is the (marginal) rate of corporate income tax.

The main drawback with this approach is that it is entirely historic: it considers the cost of existing debt with no reference to the contemporary economic climate. In the case of a company considering a new investment it would seem more logical to use the cost of new debt to the company. It can be argued on theoretical grounds that the incremental cost (i.e. the marginal cost) of taking on new debt should be considered, especially as this may cause an increase in the cost of existing debt. If the company has existing debt which it can choose to use for this particular investment (or redeem the debt), the current cost of replacement would seem the sensible option. Only if there is an existing facility with spare capacity should the historic cost of debt really be used.

Some companies prefer to subdivide their debt by maturity, and estimate separately the cost of each maturity band. This approach is, of course, perfectly sensible and acceptable, especially when considered from the viewpoint of a yield curve.

8.4   The Cost of Equity

In much the same way as the cost of debt can be obtained by "inverting" the bond valuation formula, so the cost of equity can also be obtained by "inverting" the equity valuation formula. However, this involves prognostication with regard to the stream of future dividend payments, which is fraught with difficulty. It makes sense to simplify the model by assuming the path that dividends are likely to take in the future. This can often be done by reference to the company's stated dividend payout policy, or by extrapolating the path of its recent dividend payments. One such simplifying approach is to calculate the cost of equity using (Gordon's) constant growth model (see Section 5.6.2):

$$k_e = \frac{d_1}{p_0} + g$$

$$k_e = \frac{\text{expected dividend}}{\text{present price}} + \frac{\text{expected increase in dividend}}{\text{present dividend}}$$

This suggests that the cost of equity capital (return on equity) consists of two elements: an expected dividend yield, and the growth rate of dividends. It is worth mentioning that some analysts like to distinguish between existing equity and new (or external) equity, as the latter involves the additional costs of flotation.

A second method of estimating the cost of equity capital is by use of the Capital Asset Pricing Model (CAPM):

$$k_e = \mu_f + \beta_j\left(\mu_m - \mu_f\right)$$

This formula gives the cost of equity relative to current market conditions. It assumes that the company has not changed its type of business or its size (scale) over the period of beta (β) estimation. If the company is private or does not have a long record of results, then applying this formula will be more difficult. Under such circumstances it becomes necessary to work with surrogates.

It should be noted that there are some key differences between these two approaches:

- the dividend model is forward-looking, based on expected futre dividends; CAPM looks backwards, using historical data
- the dividend model is based on fundamentals; CAPM is based on market factors.

In practice both are used, although CAPM tends to have more adherents. A recent study by Graham and Harvey (2001) discovered that some 74 per cent of companies used the CAPM to estimate the cost of capital.

It is appropriate for companies to estimate their costs on an after-tax basis. We have already seen this for the cost of debt. For the CAPM to be considered on a post-tax basis, then the pre-tax risk-free rate μ_f needs to become $\mu_f^*(1 - t)$, and the market risk premium needs to be adjusted, where t is the marginal tax rate for the firm (*not* the historic or actual tax rate).

Finally, it is worth noting that the cost of equity capital will always be greater than the cost of debt capital. This is because the cashflows from debt (interest payments, capital repayments) are much less risky from the investor perspective than the cashflows from equity (dividends, possible capital gains). Thus, investors will require a higher expected return from equity than from debt, resulting in a higher cost of equity capital from the perspective of the firm. Additionally, when one takes into account the fact that debt is typically subject to a "tax shield effect" because interest is effectively tax-deductible (see Section 8.3) then the risk premium on equity is increased in consequence.

8.5 Other Costs of Capital

Although the majority of a firm's funds tend to be financed through either debt or equity, there are some other vehicles, which we now consider.

8.5.1 The cost of retained earnings

There is a "tradition" whereby some people argue that the cost of retained earnings is zero; i.e. retained earnings are a free source of funds. However, this makes little sense in reality as retained earnings still belong to the shareholders, and their use (retention) imposes on shareholders an opportunity cost. In theory, it is possible to make the case that a company should distribute all of its earnings back to shareholders in the form of dividends, and simultaneously appeal to them for more funds, at the cost of equity capital. However, this could only be done at substantial cost in both time and money. Thus, while this approach has an intuitive theoretical appeal, in practice the main reason why (at least some) earnings are retained is to avoid the expense and delay such a procedure would entail. This does not prevent some shareholders from arguing that companies *appear* to act as if retained earnings are free! The key cost advantages of retained earnings over complete distribution of profits accompanied by newly-issued equity are:

- no issue and flotation expenses
- no taxation of dividends
- removal of the issue of any discount on newly-issued shares relative to the current share price.

In an analogous manner, it has been argued that depreciation is also a source of funds, and should be treated in a similar way to retained earnings. The purpose of depreciation is to record (in one way or another) the expiration of an earlier investment. Therefore depreciation essentially is revenue being put aside to maintain the existing structure of the company, and does not represent the method of originally funding the investment. Thus, depreciation is not a free source of funds, unless the decision has been made not to maintain the structure, and should not be included in the cost of financing. The usual argument is that if funds are provided from the depreciation account, they are charged at the average cost of capital, calculated using the various sources of funds.

8.5.2   The cost of preference shares

Known as "preferred stock" in the United States, preference shares are valued in much the same way as debt. The major differences between preference shares and debt in the UK are:

- debt is subject to a *tax-shield effect*, as it is effectively tax deductible; dividends on preference shares are not tax-deductible
- the interest payments on debt are a legal obligation to be met by the company, whereas dividends on preference shares are paid at the discretion of the Board of Directors. In reality, the dividend on UK preference shares is often at a fixed rate, but because dividends are paid out of profits (as with ordinary shares) payment is dependent on company profitability.

These differences mean that the cost of preferred shares need not be adjusted on an after-tax basis, but also that it may be more difficult to predict the future dividends paid on preferred shares. The essential similarity of preference shares and bonds means that we can apply a (slightly) modified version of the bond valuation formula to calculate the cost of preference share capital:

$$P_P = \sum_{t=1}^{\infty} \frac{D_t}{(1 + k_P)^t}$$

Note that, in common with ordinary shares, there is no final repayment date. However, for some fifty per cent of preference share issues there is a provision for periodic retirement or the company reserves the option to repurchase at a specified price. However, for example, suppose that the preference shares for a given company were expected to pay a fixed annual dividend for the foreseeable future, then their value could be calculated using the perpetuity formula:

$$P_P = \frac{D_P}{k_P}$$

where: P_P is the price of each preference share, D_P is the fixed annual dividend, and k_P is the required rate of return on preference shares. Rearranging this formula, we get an expression for calculating the cost of preference share capital:

$$k_P = \frac{D_P}{P_P}$$

8.6 The Total Cost of Capital

The total cost of capital informs the firm how much it will cost to raise funds by various means. The most common model used to calculate it is the Weighted Average Cost of Capital (WACC). As its name suggests, this is a weighted average of the various sources of capital, viz.

$$WACC \equiv k = \sum_i \pi_i k_i$$

where k_i are the various sources of capital, and π_i represents the corresponding "weights". Obviously $\Sigma \pi_i = 1$. Thus, if we assume that the only sources of capital are debt and equity we find

$$WACC \equiv k = \pi_e k_e + \pi_d k_d$$

where π_e is the proportion of equity in the total capital, and π_d is the proportion of debt in the total capital, and $\pi_e + \pi_d = 1$. The ratio of π_e to π_d (π_d/π_e) is known as the firm's capital structure (or debt/equity ratio).

If we wished to include (e.g.) preference shares as a source of capital then this would extend to

$$WACC \equiv k = \pi_e k_e + \pi_d k_d + \pi_p k_p$$

where π_p represents the proportion of capital raised via preference shares, and $\pi_e + \pi_d + \pi_p = 1$.

We have already considered how to calculate the various component costs of capital, k_e, k_d and k_p. We now need to consider how the weights (π_i) are to be estimated. The formulas typically used are

$$\pi_e = \frac{E}{D + E}, \text{ and } \pi_d = \frac{D}{D + E}$$

where

> E = value of equity (including premium accounts, retained earnings, etc)
> $\qquad$ = [ordinary shares issued]*[current market price]
> D = value of medium- and long-term debt (i.e., generally not working capital)
> $D+E$ = total value of debt and equity (= value of the firm)

In most cases it is preferable to use the market values for each of these items. This is especially the case if WACC is being used as a discount rate to assess *future* activities. This assumes that both the debt and equity markets are efficient, and that the company has both its debt and equity listed. However, while it may well be the case that large companies have their equity and some of their debt listed, they will also have some fraction of their debt which is not marketable (e.g. some forms of bank debt). On the other hand, small businesses are unlikely to have any of their securities listed.

In cases where there is no market valuation of either debt (or part thereof) or equity available, then companies and analysts will then make use of book (historic) values. This is also the case if the company is more interested in measuring the value of existing investments or past performance.

Although theory suggests that one should not mix book and market values in calculating WACC, the practicality is that quite often market values tend to be employed for equity and book values employed for debt. This occurs because of a confusion: while the concept of a varying value of equity through the share price is well understood, the fact that debt also has a varying value for a given level of future interest payments is not so well comprehended.

It is worth noting that there is a strong implicit assumption in the WACC that the current level of leverage (however measured) will continue. That is to say that any new investment will be funded using the pre-existing mix of debt and equity. There is no reason why this should be the case. In theory, one should use the WACC of existing capital (debt and equity) to calculate the existing value of the firm or an existing project. However, for new projects being considered one should use the WACC of the new capital being sought in order to undertake valuation for capital budgeting. This is not necessarily quite so simple in practice, as many investment projects are financed in part or in whole from existing funds, in which case it is impossible to identify the precise mix of debt and equity. Furthermore, fund-raising seldom occurs simultaneously for debt and equity; rather it occurs sequentially, so that the leverage (or leverage ratio) is frequently fluctuating.

One alternative is to use the Marginal Cost of Capital (MCC), which considers the marginal cost of new capital (both debt and equity) and includes both the cost of raising the new money and any cost or benefit on the market value of the existing financing. In theory this can be calculated from

$$\begin{pmatrix} \text{total cost of all financing} \\ \text{including new investment} \end{pmatrix} - \begin{pmatrix} \text{total cost of old financing} \end{pmatrix}$$

In practice the MCC is seldom used unless the new investment is so large as to affect the entire company fundamentally.

Finally, the question arises as to how the other costs associated with raising capital should be treated? These would typically include the costs of flotation, such as legal and accounting fees and commissions, stock exchange fees, advertising costs, printing costs for prospectuses, etc. Such costs do not form part of the WACC, as they do not represent the opportunity cost of capital *per se*. Nonetheless, these costs do constitute part of the cash flows of the project itself, which is how they should be treated.

We can now proceed to consider how the cost of capital might vary with changes in the firm's capital structure (its debt-equity ratio), and therefore how this might affect the value of the firm. We need to consider if changes in the amount of debt financing are likely to affect the cost of debt, and possibly even the cost of equity, thereby impacting on the WACC.

9.   The Capital Structure Conundrum

The capital structure of a company refers to the proportions of debt and equity that are used as (external) sources of funds. The capital structure may be measured by one of two ratios:

- the debt/equity ratio
- the debt/total assets ratio

Previously we considered debt and equity separately as sources of corporate funds, and examined their weighted average cost (WACC) under the implicit assumption that the amounts of debt and equity were fixed. Because the value of the firm is the discounted value of its expected future stream of earnings, and given that the objective of the company is to maximise the long-run value of the equity of the firm, then it may be argued that this can only be achieved if funds are obtained at the lowest overall long-run cost. In other words, the value of the firm is maximised when WACC is minimised. This leads to two crucial questions:

1. Is there any relationship between the capital structure of a company and the cost of the individual sources of funds?
2. Does there exist an "optimal" capital structure, such that the overall cost of funds is minimised?

9.1   Value maximisation

As we have seen throughout this book, the value of an asset is the discounted value of its future stream of earnings. This is as true for the firm as it is for securities such as debt or equity, or for a capital investment project. Indeed, it can easily be argued that a firm is essentially a portfolio of its capital investment projects. It follows, therefore, that the value of the firm will depend in part on the discount rate applied to the stream of cashflows it generates. The discount rate normally applied is the firm's weighted average cost of capital (WACC).

9.2   The "Traditional" View

At its simplest, the traditional view suggests that a firm's leverage (as measured by its debt/equity ratio) is significant in determining its cost of capital, and in consequence will affect the value of the firm. Thus, if we begin with a firm entirely financed by equity, as it acquires increasingly more debt it will find its cost of capital diminish up to a point, after which it will increase. This means that there will be a debt/equity ratio which gives the lowest WACC, at which point the value of the firm will be maximised for a given stream of cashflows. Diagrammatically this appears as follows:

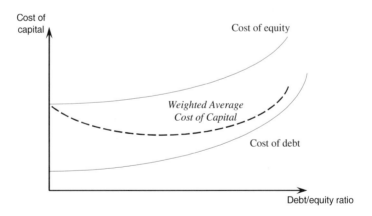

The rationale for this U-shaped WACC curve is quite straightforward: because the cost of debt is typically lower than the cost of equity, increasing leverage will initially act to lower the weighted average cost of capital. However, further increases in debt will raise the cost of capital due to increasing risk: both (potential) external providers of funds and current shareholders will seek higher return on their funds to compensate them for the increased risk of additional debt.

To examine the traditional view in a little more detail, consider the position of a company funded solely by equity. Here, the cost of capital is the cost of equity. Now, suppose the leverage (leverage) of the company is increased slightly as the company acquires a little debt. Then, according to the WACC, the cost of capital will decrease because

1. The post-tax cost of debt is less than the cost of equity (as explained earlier): $k_d^* < k_e$.
2. The cost of equity has remained constant.

It is the second assumption which is crucial. From the CAPM perspective, the cost of equity depends upon the riskiness or variability of the expected rate of return. In general, the expected return from an investment increases as the level of risk increases. Thus, as the company moves from zero leverage to a small, positive level, the shareholders' perceived risk increases. This is because by law interest has to be paid out from gross earnings irrespective of the financial fortunes of the company, hence the variability of profit-after-tax (PAT) must increase with the leverage of the company. Further, if the company goes into liquidation, debtholders take priority over equityholders. Thus the risk of an equity investment increases with leverage for these two reasons. This suggests that as the company's leverage increases (even by a small amount) the cost of equity should also increase. However, the traditional view argues that, in practice, *for low levels of leverage shareholders do not perceive any increase in their risk*. Thus the second assumption is acceptable as a matter of practicality.

Nonetheless, as the level of debt increases further then eventually shareholders will start to become concerned about their risks, and their required return will rise to compensate them accordingly. Also, as debt (and leverage) increases further still, debtholders themselves become increasingly nervous and require greater return.

Taking the views of debtholders and shareholders together, the foregoing shows the traditional view that as a function of leverage, the cost of capital first decreases with at low leverage levels and then increases with the level of leverage. The implication is that there is an optimal level of leverage corresponding to a minimum cost of capital. Trying to find this optimal debt/equity ratio which corresponds to the minimum WACC is another matter altogether.

9.3   Modigliani and Miller (1958)

While the "traditional view" of capital structure has a certain intuitive appeal, Franco Modigliani and Merton H. Miller (MM) were the first to offer a rigorous scientific analysis of the relationship between leverage and the cost of capital, and hence the value of the firm. Their 1958 paper showed that contrary to the "traditional view", the cost of capital was independent of the firm's leverage. Their analysis was based on a series of assumptions—which some consider rather restrictive—which permitted full arbitrage to occur:

1. There exist perfect capital markets, where companies and individuals can borrow without limit at the same rate of interest.
2. There are no taxes or transactions costs.
3. Personal and corporate borrowing are perfect substitutes.
4. Other firms exist having the same business (systematic) risk, but different leverage.
5. All projects, cash flows, debt, etc, can be regarded as perpetuities.

On an intuitive level, MM argued that the value of the firm—like the value of any other asset—depended upon the capitalised value of the income stream the firm generated by its activities, rather than by the manner in which its activities were financed. Thus, there is a separation of the investment decision from the financing decision. Their argument can be outlined as follows:

- Given perfect markets, shareholders perceive an increase in their risk even at very low levels of leverage
- Consequently they will demand an increased return by way of compensation.
- Because of the existence of arbitrage (assumption 3 above), this increased return will *exactly* offset the benefits to the firm of cheaper debt, thereby keeping the average cost of

capital constant, and equal to the required rate of return on equity of an ungeared company:

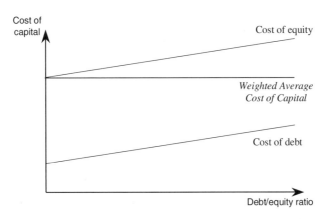

Example:

Consider two companies in the same (business) risk class: Jennings Ltd and Clemence Ltd. Both companies have annual earnings before interest of £1 million, but they have different capital structures. The companies are valued on the market as follows:

	Jennings Ltd.	Clemence Ltd.
Equity	£5,000,000	£4,000,000
Debt @ 8%	–	£2,000,000
	£5,000,000	£6,000,000

Now, suppose Bill Brown owns 5% of Clemence's equity. Ignoring taxes, his annual income would be calculated as follows:

Earnings of Clemence Ltd.		£1,000,000
less interest (8% of £2m)		£160,000
		£840,000
Bill Brown's income = 840,000 * 5% =		£42,000

Now, suppose Bill Brown sold his equity for £200,000 (= 5%*£4m), and then borrowed £100,000 from the market to maintain his financial risk at the same level. If he then bought 6% of Jennings Ltd with the £300,000, his annual earnings would become:

Earnings from Jennings Ltd.	£60,000
(£1,000,000 * 6%)	
less interest payable	£8,000
(£100,000 @ 8%)	
Bill Brown's income =	£52,000

It therefore seems that Bill Brown can increase his return while maintaining his exposure to business and financial risk.

The original theory expounded by Modigliani and Miller would claim that this result is untenable. After all, if Bill Brown can increase his return, then other investors are also likely to note and take advantage of this situation. The forces of the (perfect) market would ensure that arbitrage would occur. Ultimately this will drive down the value of Clemence's equity and push up the value of Jennings' equity until the value of the two firms became identical. Thus, under the theory of Modigliani and Miller, the value of the firm (i.e., the sum of total equity plus total market value of debt) is independent of the capital structure of the firm:

To reiterate, the key implication is that the ratio of debt to equity is irrelevant. It does not matter in what proportions the firm seeks to obtain its funding.

9.3.1 Criticisms of Modigliani and Miller

The view expounded by Modigliani and Miller in 1958 has come in for some severe criticism, not least because of the restrictive set of assumptions under which it is predicated. Additionally, the empirical evidence suggests that Boards of Directors do *not* consider their debt/equity ratio to be irrelevant.

The perfect market assumption has come in for criticism by some, although others recognise such a critique as being methodologically sound. The assumption of perfect markets is widely used in theoretical models in finance, partly because imperfect markets produce intractable models, and the assumption offers a starting point from which practical imperfections may be added afterwards.

It is also the case that many of the critics of Modigliani and Miller also make use of the Capital Asset Pricing Model (CAPM), conveniently ignoring the fact that it too is the product of a perfect markets assumption!

However, regardless of the many criticisms it has faced, the original theory expounded by Modigliani and Miller is important for several reasons. In the first instance, it has formed the basis for much theoretical thinking in financial management. Indeed, the original model has been modified to take account of less restrictive assumptions, some of which we consider below. Further, it has led to an ongoing debate on the importance of the firm's capital structure, a debate in which "the jury is still out".

9.3.2 MM Modifications

The original theory of Modigliani and Miller has subsequently been modified to take into account some of the more relevant criticisms which it faced. Most importantly, in light of the tax-shield effect (see Section 8.3), it has been redeveloped to include corporate taxation:

value of firm = value with no taxes + PV(tax shield on interest)

This implies that as the value of the firm without taxes is independent of its leverage (leverage), and given that the value of the tax-shield increases *ad infinitum* with the level of debt, companies should undertake the highest level of leverage possible, as this would maximise the value of the firm. Graphically this would appear as follows:

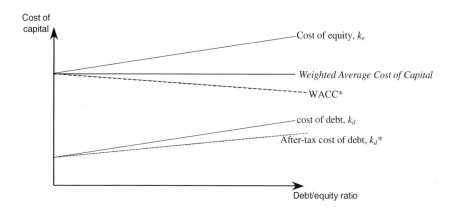

Inclusion of corporate taxation gives rise to the new after-tax cost of debt curve, k_d^*, (dotted line) which has a shallower slope than its original pre-tax variant, k_d (solid line). This lower cost of debt gives rise to an amended weighted average cost of capital curve, WACC* (dotted line), which is downward sloping. The key implication is that the more debt the firm acquires, the lower will be its weighted average cost of capital and hence the higher the value of the firm. If this were true, then it would make sense for firms to borrow as much as possible. Lenders would also realise this, and seek to lend as much as possible to enance corporate value. This is obviously not the way things operate in the real world!

The reason is very simple: this analysis result neglects to include the costs of financial distress, i.e. the cost of potential bankruptcy that occurs with increasing debt. As leverage (leverage) increases, suppliers of funds, general trade creditors, customers, etc, become increasingly nervous about dealing with the company. In particular they will be worried about the company's ability to meet its interest and debt (principal) repayments. This will manifest itself in lost sales, loss of goodwill, etc. Shareholders will also view such potential losses as an increasing threat, which serves to reduce the value of the firm. Incorporating the costs of financial distress gives:

value of firm = value with no taxes + PV(tax shield on interest)
− PV(costs of financial distress)

which suggests (again) that there is an optimum leverage level which minimises the cost of capital, and maximises the value of the firm. Graphically, this might appear as:

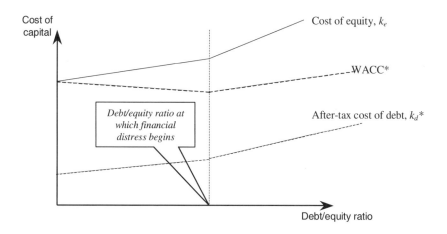

Both the cost of debt and cost of equity curves now "kink" upwards at the point at which the costs of financial distress begin. This gives rise to a V-shaped weighted average cost of capital curve, which leads to the same conclusion as the traditional viewpoint, with which we began this discussion!

In 1977 Merton Miller took the debate a stage further by introducing personal taxation into the model. In essence, Miller brought into play a "clientele effect", suggesting that the tax benefits of debt for any particular firm depends on the personal tax positions of both its shareholders and its debtholders (lenders). The implication is that firms will tend to attract investors who are "suited" to the firm's existing capital structure. If this were so, then it would make sense for firms to try to maintain their existing capital structure, as any changes might act as an incentive for shareholders and debtholders to sell their securities in the firm.

9.4   A Final Thought

This area is often one of the most unsatisfying especially for those studying finance for the first time, as there really are no definite conclusions. "The jury is still out". It is also the case that most of the work in this area is based on the assumption that the firm is a "price-taker" (an implication of the perfect markets assumption), and faces whatever costs of capital the market serves up. This is typically extended to the implicit assumption that there is no change in the market costs over time (a simplifying assumption). However, even casual observation suggests that firms will determine the form in which they raise new capital based on current and anticipated market conditions. It may therefore be the case that changes in a company's cost of capital have more to do with market conditions, both now and in the future, than anything else. Nonetheless, that also makes it one of the most fruitful areas for consideration, and a subject in which there remains a great deal of research to be done, both in theory and in practice.

10.   Extending the Focus: Some Applications

In the previous chapters of this book we have examined some of the basic tools and ideas which have established themselves as part of the toolbox of finance. In some cases ideas such as Net Present Value (NPV) have become tools which themselves are tried, tested and trusted. In other cases there is still an ongoing debate, such as we saw in the previous chapter on Modigliani and Miller's view of the relevance of the debt-to-equity ratio. In this chapter, to bring our journey to something of a close, we consider some more advanced applications of the tools and ideas which we have previously examined.

10.1   Valuation of the Firm

In earlier chapters valuation techniques such as NPV were applied to the valuation of bonds, shares, and investment projects (capital budgeting). Given that a firm is often considered as a portfolio of the investment projects it has decided to undertake, it would seem a straightforward enough matter to apply NPV techniques and be able to value the firm itself. Finance theory clearly states that the value of an asset is the discounted value of the stream of cash flows to which that asset gives rise, so the value of a firm should be the discounted value of the cash flows which the firm generates. But to which stream of cash flows should the NPV technique be applied for valuation of a company? As we have already seen, purely from the shareholders' perspective we should consider the NPV of the future stream of dividend payments. But this is from the perspective of a single stakeholder. Finance theory would seem to indicate that we should be calculating the present value of the cash flows derived from all of the company's earnings (profits), whether distributed as dividends or retained for reinvestment within the firm. In truth, the value of the firm is best calculated using the discounted value of its forecasted free cash flows.

10.1.1 Free cash flows

Free cash flow is typically defined as the **cash not retained and reinvested** in the firm. Of course, cash not retained and reinvested is cash paid out as dividends. Thus, the dividend per share is equal to free cash flow per share. As an alternative, free cash flow can be defined as the amount of cash a firm can pay out to investors after paying for all the investments necessary for growth. Thus

$$\text{Free cash flow (FCF)} = \text{revenues} - \text{costs} - \text{investments}$$

where **investments** represents the firm's spending on capital equipment (including property), which is sometimes referred to as "capital expenditures". Because the [revenues – costs] represent the firm's operating cash flow, the free cash flow can also be written as

$$\text{FCF} = \text{Operating Cash Flow (OCF)} - \text{investments}$$

Note that it is entirely possible for a rapidly-growing business to have a negative free cash flow. This would arise when the firm is engaged in a high level of capital expenditure.

In many ways, free cash flow is similar to earnings, except that FCF omits "book entry" (i.e. non-cash) expenses, and accounts for capital spending when it actually occurs rather than depreciating it over several years. The major difference between earnings and free cash flow is that depreciation accounts for sunk costs of the past, whereas free cash flow is tries to capture all of the real cash outlays of the present. In many ways, the free cash flow of a company represents a real measure of value added, but its use as an analytic device needs to be used with caution. It would be a mistake to judge a company purely on its FCF, without any regard to its level of capital investment, in particular.

10.1.2 EVA and MVA

Also known as residual value, Economic Value Added (EVA) is a proprietary concept defined by the consulting firm Stern-Stewart, and is closely equivalent to the concept of economic profit (which differs considerably from the accounting concept of profit), which is defined as the return a business makes on invested capital, minus the cost of capital times the amount of invested capital.

EVA is a measure of the surplus value created by an investment, or by a firm (which is a portfolio of the investments it undertakes). Thus

EVA = (return on capital − cost of capital)*(capital invested in project)

where **return on capital** is the true cash flow return on capital, and the **cost of capital** is the weighted average of the costs of the various funding instruments used to finance the investment.

It is also possible to define EVA as the "after-tax cash flow generated by a business minus the cost of the capital it has deployed to generate that cash flow" (cf. the definition of economic profit above). It is therefore apparent that EVA underlies true shareholder value. Note that EVA is measured in currency terms (e.g. pounds, euros, or dollars) and not in percentage terms. EVA is close both in underlying theory and construction to the NPV of a capital budgeting project.

We can make use of EVA to calculate a valuation for the firm. The present value of a firm can be written in terms of the EVA of those projects already in place and the present value of the EVA of future projects. Thus:

Value of Firm = Value of Assets in Place + Value of Future Growth

= [Investment in Existing Assets + NPV$_{\text{Assets in Place}}$] + NPV$_{\text{future projects}}$

$$= \left[I + NPV_{\text{Assets in place}} \right] + \sum_{j=1}^{N} NPV_j$$

where I is the capital invested in assets in place and there are expected to be N projects yielding surplus value (or excess returns) in the future.

10.2 Corporate Restructuring: Mergers and Acquisitions

In Chapter One we examined the relationships between the various stakeholders of the firm and considered the issue of agency costs. One of the ways in which companies try to bring the objectives of management into some kind of consistency with those of the shareholders is via their compensation package. This represents an internal form of corporate control. Nonetheless, there are also mechanisms external to the firm which can act to try to ensure managers act in the best interests of their shareholders. This array of possibilities is sometimes referred to as the market for corporate control, and consists of the possibility of various kinds of merger or acquisition (takeover). In any event, a merger or takeover should only occur if there is a strong expectation that the new entity will be greater than the sum of its individual parts. In other words, a merger or takeover *should* result in value being added, either because of synergies or of improved management. Naturally, it should be noted that expectations are not always met, so that the reality may be better or worse.

A merger refers to the friendly process of combining two (or more) separate companies into a new, single entity. Usually, the various Boards of Directors will have negotiated the mutual benefits they believe will accrue as a result of the merger before making a recommendation to shareholders for approval. Typically, the shares of one company will be exchanged for the shares of the other at a rate commensurate with their relative market prices. There are three basic kinds of merger:

1. A **horizontal merger** occurs when two firms in the same line of business combine. Such a merger can become the subject of monopoly enquiries, especially when it concerns two already large firms. One of the key motives for such a merger is the belief that it will yield economies of scale benefits. Economies of scale occur when a firm can operate at increasingly lower per unit costs as it produces increasingly more. Economies of scale are the underlying rationale for the production line method of production, so favoured by manufacturing.

2. A **vertical merger** is one in which (e.g.) a company merges with one of its suppliers, or vice versa. Essentially, vertical integration brings both supply of and demand for given products within a single company. Proponents argue that it enables better control and coordination than might otherwise be the case. But the reality is that this can only be the case if there is some kind of market failure. In

recent years vertical integration has fallen into disfavour, with companies increasingly resorting to outside suppliers of goods and services outside of their core competencies. This use of the market has become known as outsourcing.

3. A **conglomerate merger** is any merger which does not fall into either of the above categories. More specifically, it involves the combination of two firms in entirely different lines of business. It represents diversification within a company (the merged entity). Such diversification is usually considered to be a dubious motive as it can be achieved in a less costly way by individual investors adjusting (diversifying) their own share portfolios.

An acquisition or takeover occurs when one company purchases another. The purchased company can be subsumed into the buying company, in a similar manner to a merger. Alternatively, the purchased company can remain in its previous identity, and effectively be a subsidiary of the purchasing company.

In the past decade, there has also been an increasing history of divestitures and spinoffs, under which firms seek to sell off parts of their business. Spinoffs have been noticeable among the high-tech end of companies, with the more advanced units within a company often being spun off to free them from the corporate constraints that exist within the existing (large) company. In such cases, the parent company will maintain some degree of ownership through a significant shareholding in the newly independent entity. It is also sometimes the case that a firm will divest itself of units which are outside its area of core competence, perhaps describing them as being of "poor fit" with the firm's strategic direction.

Another rationale for merger or acquisition activity is the existence of surplus funds. Finance theory suggests that if a firm has fully exploited all possible investment projects and still finds itself with cash, these funds—being surplus to requirements—should be returned to the shareholders, either through a share buyback or by a bonus dividend. In practice this is not always the case, with managers seeking to enhance their own reputations (or generally believing they are doing some good for the firm) by using the surplus cash for a cash-funded merger or takeover. In part, there is an incentive for this kind of activity, as cash-rich firms are often seen as takeover targets, with the cash surplus acting as a "honey pot".

10.2.1   Leveraged buyouts (LBOs)

There are two key differences between a leveraged buyout (LBO) and the more normal kind of acquisition:

1. A large proportion of the financing of the purchase price is financed using debt. It is quite often the case that such debt is considered as "junk". Although the term can be viewed as pejorative, in this context "junk" implies nothing more than the fact that the bonds are rated below investment grade (see Table 4 in Section 4.1) due to the risk involved.
2. The shares in the LBO are removed from being traded on the open market; they are effectively private shares.

Quite often, the shares in an LBO are held privately by a small group of investors. These are typically institutional investors, i.e. financial institutions. In some cases, the LBO is arranged by the company's management, in which case it is referred to as a Management Buyout (MBO).

10.2.2   Mergers and macroeconomics

10.2.2.1   Merger Waves

History shows that merger activity tends to come in waves. There are short periods of history when merger activity occurs in abundance. Merger waves seem to occur most when share prices are buoyant, something which itself tends to occur towards the top of an economic boom (the top of the macroeconomic business cycle). In the United States there have been merger waves at the very beginning of the twentieth century, then again in the 1920s, between 1967 and 1969 as well as during the stock market boom years during the 1980s and the 1990s. Although there is a distinct correlation between share prices and merger waves researchers have found it hard to ascribe reasons.

Certainly, when the stock market is booming there is a greater possibility for shares in some companies to be considered as overvalued, making them prime targets for takeover or merger activity. It is also the case that high share prices may lead even the most rational of analysts to be swayed by the buoyant value of the merged entity, which could ultimately turn out to be overvalued when the stock market boom recedes.

10.2.3 Merger evaluation

From the foregoing, it should be clear that as with any form of investment, the key to a merger or acquisition's success is its ability to generate added value. In other words, are the two firms worth more as a single entity than separately? Expressed mathematically, we might write

Estimated gain from merger or acquisition =

PV(net accrued benefits) − cost of merger or acquisition

The net accrued benefits refer to the extra revenues or reduced costs which are expected as a result of the merger or acquisition. Their estimation is often the hardest part of the entire calculation. In a takeover, the more important calculation is to determine a reasonable value of the target firm (the subject of the takeover bid). For a company whose shares are listed on a stock exchange, it might seem that the value of the company should be the price of the shares multiplied by the number of shares. However, it is unlikely that such a price, if offered, would be attractive to existing shareholders of the target company. It is for this reason that we often note the share price of takeover targets rising substantially. Indeed, this can even be the case when the takeover is little more than a rumour, but then in efficient markets all information—even unsubstantiated rumour—is discounted into the current price.

Because a merger or takeover requires the compliance of both sets of shareholders, it is important that the benefits can be shown to accrue to both sets of shareholders. Some of this will be embodied in the complex (legal) terms under which the merger or acquisition is drafted.

Additionally, not all of the benefits and costs can be easily determined in monetary terms. One key example is that of bringing together the managers from two different corporate cultures, which has often been noted as a major source of post-merger difficulty. When the merger or takeover is cross-border, involving companies in different countries, these difficulties are typically even worse.

10.2.3.1   Winners and Losers

The primary aim of any company is to maximise returns to the shareholders. In theory, then, we ought to find that a merger generates increased benefits to the shareholders of both firms involved, while a takeover benefits the shareholders of both the acquiring firm and the acquired firm. At the very least, we ought to find that a merger or takeover generates enough benefits overall that the losses sustained by some shareholders will be outweighed by the gains of the other group of shareholders. The evidence suggests that shareholders of a firm which is the subject of a takeover bid are likely to be winners, at least in the short-run.

10.2.3.2   Tactics

There are a number of methods by which one company can make an offer to merge or acquire another:

1. Friendly discussions between the acquiring company and the target;
2. The acquiring firm goes directly to the shareholders of the target firm with a tender offer.

In the latter case, the takeover is often referred to as "hostile". Companies which are takeover targets, or believe they are potential targets, have several means at their disposal for trying to deter or prevent the hostile takeover:

1. **The poison pill**: this refers to any tactic employed by the target firm to avoid being acquired. Such measures could include offering existing shareholders the right to buy additional shares at an attractive price if the acquiring company has a large shareholding.

2. **The white knight**: often the target company may have in mind being acquired by a different company from the firm which has already made its acquisitive aspirations known. The friendly potential acquirer is referred to as a white knight.
3. **Shark repellent**: this refers to changes made to the company's Memorandum and Articles of Association (or in the USA, corporate charter) in order to prepare to defend against hostile takeovers. One such common repellent is to amend the Memorandum so that a takeover requires approval by a supermajority of (e.g.) 80 per cent of shareholders, rather than the more common simple majority (51 per cent).

10.3 Pensions

In the past pensions have often been little more than an appendix to the mainstream body of corporate finance. In the modern era this is no longer the case. Although an occupational pension fund is legally a separate entity from the (parent) company, any financial pressures on the pension fund will also affect the company. It is also the case that in the past (parent) companies have found themselves beneficiaries from exceptional performance by the pension fund.

Nowadays, many companies have been adversely affected by the financial position of their pension fund. The combined effects of an ageing population together with an equities market which has been in decline for a few years has meant that pension funds have been paying out more money to pensioners, and receiving in less money both by way of contributions from working members and less money from investment income. This problem largely affects **defined benefit** (DB) pension funds, which have traditionally been the major form of pension fund in the UK. These are pension schemes which promise workers in advance a specific monthly benefit upon retirement based on their earnings and the number of years in service. Regardless of the investment performance of the pension fund, these benefits have to be met. Thus, during years of poor investment performance it is sometimes necessary for employers to make top up contributions to the pension fund, which may be in actuarial deficit. During the good years of investment performance, the pension fund may find itself in actuarial surplus, so that the employer can reclaim some of the surplus, either directly or via a "contributions holiday", in which the employer makes no further contributions for a period of time. Under a defined benefit scheme almost all of the risk falls upon the parent company employer. The demographic shift to an ageing population and the poor performance of the capital markets has meant that defined benefit schemes have become increasingly unattractive to employers, with many companies closing their DB schemes to new entrants, and establishing **defined contribution** (DC) schemes instead.

Also known as **money purchase** schemes, DC schemes do not promise workers any predetermined benefits. Rather the worker's pension will depend on (i) the contributions made into the fund on his or her behalf (usually made by both employer and employee), and (ii) the investment returns earned on those monies. Under a DC scheme, the risk is borne by the workers. DC schemes are less affected by the demographic shifts, but the pensions paid are entirely dependent upon the state of the capital markets in which the fund is invested.

While the majority of DB (and DC) pension funds have tried to "sit tight" during the recent decline in the capital markets and the demographic shift to an ageing population, the problem for the parent companies has recently been exacerbated by changes in the way in which companies account for their pension liabilities.

10.3.1   FRS 17

FRS 17 is an accounting standard designed to show on an annual basis the cost of a company's commitment to fund employee pensions. Similar to America's FAS 87, it has been praised by some for introducing "valuable consistency and transparency". Since it came into full force in June 2003, there has been a succession of bad news stories showing the severe underfunding of many of the pension funds of the UK's top companies. Before the introduction of FRS 17, UK companies accounted for their pension liabilities under the SSAP 24 accounting standard, which allowed companies to "smooth" their pension liabilities over several years. On the other hand, FRS 17 requires annual disclosure of pension fund's surplus or deficit, making it more subject to the vagaries of the performance of the capital markets. One of the key criticisms of FRS 17 is that it is essentially a short-term measure, forcing companies to take short-term actions on their pension funds, which might conflict with longer-term objectives. It also has the impact of making annual accounts more volatile than would otherwise have been the case. Additionally, it is also true that in 2005 the UK has already committed itself to adopt an international standard on accounting for pension liabilities, bringing the decision to implement FRS 17 under both economic and political criticism. It will be interesting to see how companies continue to react to this new accounting standard, as well as to its successor in 2005.

10.4   Finance in the International Arena

Nowadays, businesses of every size are increasingly involved in international transactions. The world has truly become business' oyster! One medium that has made international trade all the more accessible has been the Internet. Even a small business that has traditionally focused on a local market can now sell to overseas customers who can access its website. Additionally, the increasing credibility of the common European currency, the euro (€), throughout most of the countries of the European Union has given an added stimulus to cross-border transactions, because there is no need to change currencies. Thus, there is a much smaller (sometimes negligible) international finance component in intra-EU transactions. Nonetheless, such transactions have given smaller EU companies a taste for operating outside their more traditional national boundaries, encouraging them to go beyond the countries of the EU. It is apparent that international transactions are essentially of two varieties:

- International trade: this can involve either buying from abroad (importing) or selling to overseas customers (exporting), or perhaps both;

- International finance: at its broadest this involves both the purchase or sale of overseas currency, or financing activities across national boundaries (including both loan transactions and equity transactions).

Our concern is with the latter, although it should be noted that in the corporate context it is international trade which is the key driver of international finance. In many cases, the tools required for analysing international financial decisions are extensions of the same tools applied in the domestic context. We begin with an overview of the international financial markets.

10.4.1   Foreign exchange (forex or fx)

10.4.1.1   Spot Markets

In order for individuals or companies in one country to purchase goods and services from another country, they must first acquire the currency of that country. The price of the overseas currency in terms of the home country's currency is the exchange rate. If we consider the United Kingdom as the home country and (for example) the United States as the overseas country, then the exchange rate refers to how many UK pounds it takes to buy one dollar expressed as a "direct quote". An "indirect quote" would be how many US dollars it takes to buy a UK pound. The indirect quote is nothing more than the reciprocal of the direct quote. In the global foreign exchange (forex) markets most currencies tend to be quoted on an indirect basis, with the exception of the UK pound and the euro (€).

Because the exchange rate between two currencies is a price, like any other price, it is determined by the interaction of the forces of supply and demand. To a large degree the demand for any given overseas currency is a derived demand, the demand being for the underlying commodities that the currency can buy: i.e. goods, services and securities. Some element of the demand for overseas currency will be for speculative purposes. The supply of a given currency reflects demand for one or more overseas currencies; it is with "home currency" that payment is made for the overseas currency.

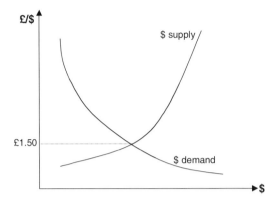

The diagram above shows the market for US dollars, priced in terms of UK £[7]. The equilibrium exchange rate is £1.40 per US $. Anything which causes either the $ demand curve or the $ supply curve to shift will bring about a change in the equilibrium exchange rate. The international demand for a given currency depends on the following factors:

- Overseas demand for "home country" products (goods and/or services)
- Overseas demand for "home country" financial assets
- Transfer payments (payments for which there is no counterbalancing transaction, such as gifts, interest or dividend payments, etc.) into the "home country"
- Speculative demand for the "home country" currency.

Thus, for example, suppose there was an increased demand for US dollars because it became more fashionable in the UK to wear US clothing. This would lead to an increased demand for US dollars to import these items into the UK. In the diagram above, the $ demand curve would shift to the right, thereby increasing the US dollar exchange rate (i.e., making the US dollar more expensive to purchase with UK

---

[7] In the foreign exchange markets each currency is denoted by a three letter symbol based on the ISO 4217 standard. Thus, UK £ usually appears as UKP, US dollars as USD, euros (€) as EUR and so on. A full listing of these codes can be found at http://www.xe.com/iso4217.htm.

pounds). The US $ would be said to have **appreciated** against the UK £; the UK £ would be said to have **depreciated** against the US $.

Because overseas currency is paid for with "home country" currency, the supply curve for a given currency is a reflection of the demand for overseas currency. Thus, the factors which shift the demand curve for overseas currency will shift the supply curve for "home country" currency, viz:

- "Home country" demand for overseas products (goods and/or services)
- "Home country" demand for overseas financial assets
- Transfer payments (payments for which there is no counterbalancing transaction, such as gifts, interest or dividend payments, etc.) out of the "home country"
- Speculative demand for overseas currency.

At the time of writing, the forex markets in London are still probably the largest by volume, with some $700 billion changing hands each day. Turnover in New York and Tokyo together is some $500 billion each day. Of this volume, the major portion is for spot exchange rate transactions, i.e. the exchange rate for an immediate exchange of currencies. However, this is not the only kind of forex transaction, as it also possible to purchase (sell) currency for delivery at some future date. Such an agreement is typically known as a forward rate agreement.

10.4.1.2   Derivatives

In general, a derivative is a contract whose value depends on the value of some underlying asset. In Chapter Five (Section 5.8) we considered equity options, whose value depended on the value of the underlying equity. In a similar manner, there are also **put** and **call options** on overseas currency. Further, there are also **forward rate agreements** and **futures** contracts on overseas currency, which we consider below. The primary use for which exchange rate derivatives were designed was to hedge exchange rate risk; that is, to reduce the impact of the volatility of exchange rate fluctuations on the company. This is not to suggest that they are not used to achieve other objectives. Indeed, it is often the case that derivatives are used in a speculative manner, to try to leverage up rates of return. When such tactics go wrong they often do so spectacularly, and it is from this perspective that a great deal of the criticism of derivatives descends.

10.4.1.2A   Forward Markets and Hedging

A forward rate agreement, or forward contract, is an agreement for the delivery of a currency at a specified time in the future, at a price specified now known as the **forward rate**. By engaging in a forward rate agreement, both counterparties are (contractually) locking themselves into a fixed price for the exchange of currencies, thereby removing the chance of any loss (also of any gain) due to future movement in the exchange rate.

A forward contract can be drawn up between any two counterparties, for any mutually agreeable size, currency, and expiration. Although there is no formal market *per se* for forward contracts, they are traded directly bank-to-bank by telephone in what is known as the **interbank market**. Transactions costs for forwards are in the form of a bid-ask spread. Because forward contracts are tailored to the needs of the two counterparties, they are typically for large transactions.

A **futures contract** is a standardised form of forward rate agreement, and essentially works in much the same manner, allowing exchange rate risk to be hedged by "locking in" the exchange rate. Standardisation comes in the form of each contract being highly uniform—in size of contract, and with standard expiration dates, usually the third Wednesday of March, June, September and December—making them more tradeable and hence more liquid than a similar forward contract. Futures contracts are typically for a much smaller size than forward contracts. Transaction costs appear in the form of commission paid to brokers; there is no bid-ask spread.

The futures market consists of a central marketplace, which includes both a primary and secondary market, as well as a clearing corporation. In London this has traditionally been euronext•LIFFE (previously LIFFE, the London International Financial Futures Exchange), while in the USA this is the International Monetary Market (IMM) division of the Chicago Mercantile Exchange. In practice, the futures contract is between the counterparty and the exchange itself. Further, futures contracts are marked-to-market on a daily basis. Effectively this means that at the close of each day's trading settlement is made between counterparties, with a new one-day contract being written for the next day. This takes place each day for the life of the futures contract, and reduces the possibility of default risk. It also makes it much easier for the counterparties to monitor their position on a day-to-day basis.

10.4.1.2B   Currency Options

Currency options are very similar to equity options, the essential difference being that the underlying asset is a currency rather than shares in a company. A currency **call option** gives the holder the right, but not the obligation, to buy the underlying currency at a specified exchange rate on or before a given date. Similarly, a currency **put option** gives the holder the right, but not the obligation, the right to sell the underlying currency. Currency options offer the ability to hedge exchange rate risk, but with added flexibility. The option offers a fixed price at which the currency can be bought (call) or sold (put) if the option is exercised, but if the underlying exchange rate unexpectedly moves in a more favourable direction then the option can be left to expire, unexercised, and the overseas currency bought or sold on the spot market at a more favourable rate.

10.4.1.2C   In Summary

The international financial markets we have been discussing in this section do not deal with matters of long-term financing. Rather they are concerned with what is referred to as **treasury management**; short-term funds management largely dealing with the management of exchange rate risk. Both futures and options can be used to help managers hedge their exchange rate risk. Ultimately, the position taken in the option or futures market depends on the position in the spot market which is being hedged. Of the two kinds of derivative, there can be no doubt that futures offer a more perfect hedge, as they "lock in" the exchange rate. However, options offer the manager a much greater degree of flexibility in the form of the ability to "walk away" if the exchange rate moves favourably, rather than unfavourably as anticipated. Options enable the manager to reduce his downside risk, yet at the same time allow him the ability to take advantage of any upside potential. Such flexibility comes at a price, with the option typically being more expensive than the futures approach.

10.4.1.3 Euromarkets and others

In addition to the markets for foreign exchange, there are a number of other international financial markets. At the most basic level, the bond and equity markets in other countries can act as a source of international capital for the largest of companies. In addition to these there are also the euromarkets, which might more properly be referred to as xeno-markets or external-markets. A euromarket refers to the market for loans in a given currency outside the jurisdiction of the country in whose currency the loan is denominated. Thus the eurodollar market is for dollar-denominated loans outside of the United States, and therefore not subject to U.S. regulation. Indeed, the eurodollar market is the largest of the euromarkets. This lack of regulation makes the euromarkets a particularly attractive (and low-cost) institution for raising funds, despite the drawback of the extra risk entailed as a result.

10.4.1.4 Exchange rate relationships

Although one can easily make use of supply and demand curve diagrams to analyse changes in the international arena to predict the future movement of exchange rates, it is also possible to distil the bulk of the information into a handful of basic exchange rate relationships. In most cases, these relate changes in exchange rates to movements in underlying macroeconomic factors in the relevant countries. As with so many ideas within finance, the concept of arbitrage underlies much of what follows.

10.4.1.4A Purchasing Power Parity (PPP)

Absolute Purchasing Power Parity is an intuitively simple idea, suggesting that the price of a basket of goods in one country should be equivalent to the price in another country when converted via the exchange rate. Also known as "the Law of One Price" (LOOP), it is based on the simple premise that if it were not true there would be incentive for profit-seekers to buy commodities in the low-price country and then sell them in the high-price country for a riskless arbitrage profit. If such arbitrage occurred it would raise prices in the low-price country (due to increased demand) and lower prices in the high-price country (due to increased supply), thereby bringing prices across countries into a PPP equilibrium. One of the most interesting uses made of Absolute PPP is *The Economist*'s "Big Mac standard" in which the Big Mac is used as a proxy basket of goods with comparison being made between its exchange-rate adjusted price in different countries. Unsuprisingly, the price varies tremendously between countries, suggesting that Absolute PPP does not hold. But then it is virtually impossible to arbitrage the Big Mac, partly because it is perishable, and partly because it is a branded good.

While Absolute PPP is essentially a static view of the relationship between prices and the exchange rate, **Relative PPP** takes a more dynamic view. Here the suggestion is that the exchange rate should adjust to reflect changes in the price levels (inflation) of the two countries. Thus

$$Future \ spot \ = \ spot * \left[\frac{1 \ + \ inflation_A}{1 \ + \ inflation_B} \right]$$

If the inflation rate is measured on an annual basis, then this equation tells us that the spot rate one year from now (future spot) should equal the current spot rate multiplied by the ratio between the two countries' inflation rates. One of the key implications is that countries with relatively high rates of inflation should find their currencies depreciating.

10.4.1.4B   Interest Rates and Exchange Rates

In theory arbitrage should ensure that interest rates—adjusted for the exchange rate—in different countries are the same for loans of similar risk, i.e. there should be **interest rate parity**. The only difference between interest rates in different countries ought to be for the different sovereign (political) risks involved. This should happen as investors seek to maximise the return on their investment funds by placing them where they can earn the highest possible rate of return. Of course, large investors will also seek to diversify their risks by holding a portfolio of bonds from different countries. Consider, for example, an investor who can place one million pounds of investment funds in the United Kingdom, a high-income developed economy, at a rate of interest of 6 per cent or in country B, a less-developed economy, at a rate of interest of 15 per cent. The immediately obvious answer would be to opt for the higher rate of interest, *ceteris paribus*, but then other things are rarely constant. In order for the investment to be made the funds will first have to be converted into the currency of country B at a known rate of exchange. When the investment is eventually liquidated (as it must surely be at some time), the funds will need to be repatriated at the then-existing rate of exchange. That the rate of exchange is likely to be different at the end of the investment could well mean that any gain on the rate of interest could be countered by an adverse change in the exchange rate. If this were not the case then it would be a simple case to make riskless arbitrage profits by borrowing in the low-interest country and lending in the high-interest country.

The result of this maximising behaviour ought to be a clear relationship between the interest rates and exchange rates in any two countries, i.e. interest rate parity. This can be stated mathematically as:

$$\text{Forward rate} = \text{spot} * \frac{\left[1 + \text{Interest}_A\right]}{\left[1 + \text{Interest}_B\right]}$$

or, differences in interest rates are offset by differences between spot and forward exchange rates.

10.4.1.4C   Inflation and Exchange Rates

Relative PPP suggests a relationship between exchange rate movements and the relative inflation rates of any two countries. Similarly, we have just considered the relationship between interest rates and exchange rates. What we have not yet taken into account is the relationship between interest rates and inflation: the Fisher Effect (see Section 4.4). By combining the Fisher Effect with Relative PPP we obtain the **International Fisher Effect**. In one sense the International Fisher Effect is little more than an extension of the Fisher Effect to the international arena: while we would *not* expect nominal interest rates to be the same in different counties, real interest rates *should* be equal across countries. If this were not the case, there would be the possibility of arbitrage profits which, if exploited, would then serve to equalise the real rates of interest in different countries. However, it is also possible for any differences in real interest rates across countries to be compensated for (offset) by exchange rate differences. Thus:

$$\text{Future spot} = \text{spot} * \frac{\left[1 + \text{Interest}_A\right]}{\left[1 + \text{Interest}_B\right]}$$

It is apparent from this equation that currencies with high nominal interest rates (due to relatively high inflation rates) should find their currencies depreciating. This can also be stated as "the spot exchange rate should change equally but opposite to any change in interest rate differences between two economies".

Each of the three foregoing relationships can be summarised in a simple diagram:

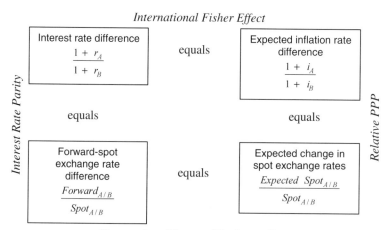

Expectations Theory of Exchange Rates

In addition there is a fourth relationship, between the forward-spot differential and the expected change in the spot exchange rate over time. This is known as the **Expectations Theory**. Bearing in mind that the future path of the exchange rate is unknown, the best guidance we have for it is the forward exchange rate (bear in mind that if the forex market is efficient, then the exchange rate will follow a random walk). The forward exchange rate essentially offers an average of the forecasts of the path of the exchange rate by all the "players" in the market.

This theory does not suggest that financial managers are able to forecast the future spot exchange rate with impeccable certainty. Rather it suggests that while forecasts will sometimes prove too low in the fullness of time, and sometimes too high, but there will be no tendency of bias in either direction. Thus, the forecasts will on average prove to be correct. Thus, on average the forward rate will equal the future spot rate.

Each and every one of these four relationships can be used as the basis for predicting exchange rates. In practice, finance departments will tend to use more sophisticated variants, and even cocktails of the above. Nonetheless, even if forex markets are efficient, it is necessary to have some means of forecasting exchange rates in order to make rational financial (business) decisions. Exchange rate forecasts help managers determine which countries to sell into (export), and which countries to buy from (import). Forecasts are also useful in assessing whether to raise capital at home or from capital markets overseas. Some forecast of the path of the relevant exchange rate is required in order to determine whether or not to use a hedging tool, such as a forward, future or option. Indeed, on the basis of the forex forecast the financial manager can determine which of these tools will best serve the needs of the firm.

10.4.2 *International capital budgeting*

In much the same way that companies conduct an exercise in capital budgeting (investment appraisal, see Chapter 6) within the confines of one country, companies which operate in more than one country will often need to undertake a similar exercise for capital expenditure across national boundaries. In either case, the best tool available is to make use of NPV calculations. One of the key questions that arises is whether the appraisal should be undertaken from the viewpoint of the project *per se* (as is typically the case with domestic capital budgeting) or from the viewpoint of the parent company? The importance of this question has to do with the fact that there are possible differences between the net cash flows of the project *per se* and those project cash flows which are available for repatriation to the parent company. The typical answer to this question is to appraise the project from the viewpoint of the parent company.

Suppose, for example, that a company is considering an expansion investment in the form of building an extra factory for production. It has two choices: build the factory at home (i.e. in the home country), or build the factory overseas (foreign direct investment, FDI). The first step would be to determine forecasts of the two sets of cash flows, but each of these would be in the relevant currency, making any immediate comparison invalid. One way of making the cash flows comparable would be to convert them into a single currency. Which currency should be used typically would depend on the currency in which the capital had been raised:

- If the funding for the project had been raised at home, then the overseas cash flows should be converted into "home currency" using forecasts of the exchange rate (or forward exchange rates, if they exist).
- If the funding for the project had been raised "locally" (i.e. overseas), then the cash flows should be converted into the overseas currency using the forecasted exchange rate (or forward rates, if they exist).
- However, if exchange rate hedging is to take place, it is possible to calculate the entire NPV in the relevant currency, then convert it at the current exchange rate.

In practice, because the parent company is often "western-originated", and therefore based in one of the more advanced, high-income economies, while the potential FDI projects are located in low- or middle-income economies, it is mostly the case that cash flows are calculated in the currency of the parent company's "home country". In some cases, the very large multinational corporations tend to conduct all of their analyses in one of the major global currencies, such as the US dollar or the euro.

10.4.2.1   International Cost of Capital

In the same way as there is an issue concerning which currency should be used for denominating investment project cash flows, there is also an issue concerning the calculation of the cost of capital for international capital budgeting. One possibility is to convert the overseas cost of capital into the domestic rate, or *vice versa*. Another possibility exists when the funds have all been raised in the domestic capital markets, in which case the company's domestic WACC is applicable.

10.5   The Limitations of Finance

The various tools of finance we have investigated in this book have an important role to play in helping corporate decision-makers come to robust and trustworthy conclusions. Nonetheless, as with any tools, the conclusions at which executives arrive are only as trustworthy as the manner in which the tools themselves are used. For a tool to operate most effectively it has to be applied in the appropriate manner: it is absurd to use sandpaper to knock a nail into a wall! The proper use of financial tools in decision-making depends on a full understanding of what the tool can deliver and where its shortcomings lie. If the decisions suggested by the use of financial tools were infallible, there would be no need for any human input; we could programme a computer to apply the relevant financial tools to the corporate and market data that come in. We would be able to successfully run a business using only computer-generated decisions. My own view is that one should not become overly reliant on the tools of finance, but to use them and their output as one important element—guidance—for decision-making. The actual decision should be made partly on the basis of the objective advice proffered by using the financial tool combined with an element of judgement, which ought to come primarily from experience and is therefore subject to a degree of subjectivity.

It has been the aim of this book to try to bring the basics of finance to the reader in a focused and readable manner. I hope I have whetted your appetite for an exciting and ever-evolving field of both study and practice.

Bibliography

Accounting Standards Committee. 1975.

Bachelier, Louis. 1900. "Théorie de la spéculation". *Annales Scientifiques de l'Ecole Normale Superieure*, III-17, 21-86. (English translation by A. J. Boness in P. H. Cootner (ed.) 1967. *The Random Character of Stock Market Prices*. Cambridge MA: MIT Press

Bernoulli, D. 1738. "Exposition of a new theory on the measurement of risk". Translated by L. Sommer, *Econometrica* **22** January 1954 23–36

Black, F. and M. Scholes. 1973. "The pricing of options and corporate liabilities". *Journal of Political Economy* **81**(3) May–June: 637–654

Blume, Friend and Westerfield. 1980. *US survey: Impediments to Capital Formation*

Bromwich, Michael. 1976. *The Economics of Capital Budgeting*. Harmondsworth, Middlesex: Penguin Books

Coase, R. H. 1937. "The nature of the firm". *Economica* 386–405

Clayton, G. 1962. "British financial intermediaries in theory and practice", *Economic Journal* **72**: December 869-886

Clayton, G. and Osborn, W. T. 1965 *Insurance Company Investment: Principles and Policy*. London: Allen and Unwin.

Cowles, A. 1933. "Can stock market forecasters forecast?" *Econometrica* **1**(3): July 309–324

Cox, J., J. Ingersoll, Jnr. and S. Ross. 1981. "A re-examination of traditional hypotheses about the term structure of interest rates". *Journal of Finance* **36** (4) September: 769–799

Cox, J., J. Ingersoll, Jnr. and S. Ross. 1985. "A theory of the term structure of interest rates". *Econometrica* **53**(2) March: 385–407

Culbertson, J. 1957. "The term structure of interest rates". *Quarterly Journal of Economics* **71** November 485–517

Dean, Joel. 1951. *Capital Budgeting*. New York: Columbia University Press

Dixit, Avinash and Robert Pindyck. 1994. *Investment Under Uncertainty.*

The Economist. (various issues)

Fisher, Irving. 1930. *The Theory of Interest.*

Gordon, M. J. 1959. "Dividends, earnings, and stock prices". *Review of Economics and Statistics* **41**: May 99–105

Graham, J. and C. Harvey, 2001, "The Theory and Practice of Corporate Finance: Evidence from the Field". *Journal of Financial Economics* **60** May/June

Hicks, J. R. 1946. *Value and Capital*, second edition. London: Oxford University Press

Hirshleifer, J. 1958. "On the theory of optimal investment decisions". *Journal of Political Economy* August

Jensen, M. C. and W. H. Meckling. 1976. "Theory of the firm: managerial behavior, agency costs and ownership structure". *Journal of Financial Economics* **3**(4): October 305–360

Kendall, M. 1953. "The analysis of economic time series. Part 1: Prices". *Journal of the Royal Statistical Society* **96**(1): 11–25

Keynes, J. M. 1921. *A Treatise on Probability*. London: Macmillan

Keynes, J. M. 1936. *The General Theory of Employment, Interest and Money*. London: Macmillan

Knight, F. H. 1921. *Risk, Uncertainty and Profit*.

Kolb, Robert W. 1985. *Understanding Futures Markets*. Scott Foresman

Laidler, D. E. W. 1985. *The Demand for Money*, third edition. Harper & Row

Lintner, J. 1965. "The valuation of risky assets and the selection of risky investments in stock portfolios and capital budgets". *Review of Economics and Statistics* **47**: February 13–37

Lorie, J. H. and L. J. Savage (October) "Three Problems in Rationing Capital". *Journal of Business*, 1955

Malkiel, B. 1966. *The Term Structure of Interest Rates: Expectations and Behavior Patterns*. Princeton: Princeton University Press

Malkiel, B. (various years) *A Random Walk Down Wall Street*. New York: Norton

Markowitz. H. M. 1952. "Portfolio selection". *Journal of Finance* **7**: March 77–91

Markowitz. H. M. 1959. *Portfolio Selection: Efficient Diversification of Investments*. New York: Wiley

Michaelsen, J. B. 1963. "The Term Structure of Interest Rates: Comment". *Quarterly Journal of Economics* February 166–174

Michaelsen, J. B. 1965. "The Term Structure of Interest Rates and Holding-Period Yields on Government Securities". *Journal of Finance* September 444–463

Miller, M. H. 1977. "Debt and taxes". *Journal of Finance* **32**(2): May 261–275

Modigliani, F. and M. H. Miller. 1958. "The cost of capital, corporation finance and the theory of investment". *American Economic Review* **48**(3) June: 261–297

Modigliani, F. and M. H. Miller. 1963. "Corporate income taxes and the cost of capital". *American Economic Review* **53** June: 433–443

Modigliani, F. and Richard Sutch. 1967. "Debt Management and the Term Structere of Interest Rates". *Journal of Political Economy* August: supplement

Mossin, J. 1966. "Equilibrium in a capital asset market". *Econometrica* **34**(4): October 768–783

Pike, R. H. and T. S. Ooi. 1988. "The impact of corporate investment objectives and constraints on capital budgeting practices." *British Accounting Review* August

Roberts, H. 1959. "Stock market 'patterns' and financial analysis: methodological suggestions". *Journal of Finance* **14**(1): March 1-10

Roberts, H. 1967. "Statistical versus clinical prediction of the stock market". Unpublished manuscript, CRSP. Chicago: University of Chicago

Ross, S. A. 1976. "The arbitrage theory of capital asset pricing". *Journal of Economic Theory* **13**(3): December 341–360

Roy, A. D. 1952 "Safety first and the holding of assets". *Econometrica* **20** July 431–449

Ryan, T. M. 1973. "The demand for financial assets by the British life funds". *Oxford Bulletin of Economics and Statistics* **35**: February 61-67

Samuelson, P. A. 1970. "The fundamental approximation theorem of portfolio analysis in terms of means, variances and higher moments". *Review of Economic Studies* **37**(4): October 537–542

Sharpe, W. 1964. "Capital asset prices: a theory of market equilbrium under conditions of risk". *Journal of Finance* **19**: September 425–442

Silber, William L. 1970. *Portfolio Behavior of Financial Institutions: An Empirical Study with Implications for Monetary Policy, Interest Rate Determination and Financial Model Building*, Holt, Rinehart & Winston, New York

Tobin, James. 1958. "Liquidity preference as behavior towards risk". *Review of Economic Studies* **25**: February 65–86

Working, H. 1934. "A random difference series for use in the analysis of time series". *Journal of the American Statistical Association* **29** March 11–24

Index